Chapter 1: Introduction to Psychodynamic Thera
- History Of Psychodynamic Therapy
- Basic Principles And Concepts
- Comparison With Other Therapies 8

.... 9

Chapter 2: Freud's Theory of the Unconscious 10
- The Id 10
- The Ego 10
- The Superego 11
- Role of Self-awareness in Psychodynamic Therapy 11
- Conclusion 12

.... 12

Chapter 3: The Therapeutic Relationship 13
- Importance of the Therapeutic Alliance 13
- Transference and Countertransference 13
- Boundaries in Therapy 14

.... 14

Chapter 4: Techniques in Psychodynamic Therapy 16
- Free Association 16
- Dream Analysis 16
- Projective Tests 17
- Incorporating Techniques into Therapy 17
- In Conclusion 18

.... 18

Chapter 5: Understanding Psychodynamic Assessment 19
- Psychodynamic Diagnostic Manual 19
- Developing a Psychodynamic Formulation 19
- Case Conceptualization 20
- Conclusion 20

.... 21

Chapter 6: Childhood and Developmental Issues 22
- Freud's Psychosexual Stages 22
- Psychodynamic Understanding of Attachment 23
- Impact of Childhood Experiences on Adult Functioning 23

.... 24

Chapter 7: Defense Mechanisms 25
- Types of Defense Mechanisms 25
- Role in Coping with Stress 25
- Recognizing and Working with Defense Mechanisms in Therapy 25

.... 26

Chapter 8: Addressing Resistance in Psychodynamic Therapy 27
- Understanding Resistance 27
- Reasons for Resistance 27
- Strategies for Addressing Resistance 28
- Conclusion 29

.... 29

Chapter 9: Understanding and Treating Depression, Bipolar Disorder and Psychodynamic Therapy 30
- Understanding and Treating Depression 30
- Bipolar Disorder and Psychodynamic Therapy 30
- Case Examples 31

.... 32

Chapter 10: Understanding and Treating Generalized Anxiety Disorder, Panic Disorder, OCD, and Psychodynamic Therapy 33
- Understanding and Treating GAD 33
- Understanding and Treating Panic Disorder 34
- Understanding and Treating OCD 34
- Psychodynamic Therapy and Case Examples 35

Chapter 11: Personality Disorders in Psychodynamic Therapy 36
- Types of Personality Disorders 36
- Psychodynamic Understanding and Treatment 36
- Case Examples 37
- Conclusion 37

.... 38

Chapter 12: Understanding Trauma 39
- Understanding Trauma 39
- Importance of Processing Traumatic Memories 39
- Techniques for Working with Traumatic Reactions 40

.... 40

Chapter 13: The Art of Healing Relationships 41

Understanding and Treating Relationship Issues	41
Attachment Styles and Conflict Resolution	42
Case Examples	42
In Conclusion	43
	43

Chapter 14: Family Dynamics and Interpersonal Patterns … 44
Family Dynamics and Interpersonal Patterns	44
Working with Communication and Boundaries	45
Case Examples	45
	46

Chapter 15: Psychodynamic Therapy for Children and Adolescents … 47
Adaptations of Psychodynamic Therapy for Younger Clients	47
Techniques and Considerations	47
Case Examples	48
	48

Chapter 16: Psychodynamic Therapy for Addiction … 50
Understanding Addiction from a Psychodynamic Perspective	50
Addressing Underlying Issues	50
Case Examples	51
	52

Chapter 17: Psychodynamic Therapy for Eating Disorders … 53
The Role of Early Experiences in the Development of Eating Disorders	53
Addressing Body Image and Self-esteem	53
Case Examples	54
Conclusion	55
	55

Chapter 18: Psychodynamic Therapy for Sexual Issues … 56
Understanding and Addressing Sexual Dysfunction	56
Paraphilias and Gender Identity	57
Case Examples	57
	58

Chapter 19: Integrating Cultural Competence in Psychodynamic Therapy … 59
Understanding Cultural Competence	59
Addressing Power and Privilege in the Therapeutic Relationship	59
The Importance of Cultural Humility	60

Integrating Cultural Competence in Practice...60
Challenges and Critiques..60
The Impact on the Therapist and the Client..61
Conclusion..61
....61

Chapter 20: Ethical and Professional Issues in Psychodynamic Therapy.....62
Dual Relationships..62
Self-disclosure..62
Confidentiality and Boundaries... 63
Ethical Decision-making... 63
....64

Chapter 21: Integration of Neuroscientific Findings in Psychodynamic Theory.........65
Introduction..65
Neuroscientific Contributions to Psychodynamic Theory...............................65
Implications for Practice..66
Future Directions..66
Conclusion...66
....67

Chapter 22: The Evidence for Psychodynamic Therapy..68
Research Supporting the Effectiveness of Psychodynamic Therapy..........68
Critiques and Limitations...69
Implications for Clinical Practice..69
....70

Chapter 23: Integrating Psychodynamic Therapy with Other Approaches...............71
Complementary Approaches..71
Challenges and Benefits of Integration..71
Case Examples...72
In Conclusion..73
....73

Chapter 24: The Importance of Supervision in Psychodynamic Therapy......................74
Importance of Supervision..74
Essential Skills and Competencies...75
Case Examples...75
....76

Chapter 25: Burnout Prevention and Self-care in Psychodynamic Therapy................77

Impact of Therapist's Emotional Investment..77
　　Strategies for Self-care..77
　　Case Examples..78
....79
Chapter 26: Relapse Prevention in Psychodynamic Therapy...80
　　Understanding Vulnerabilities and Triggers..80
　　Developing an Aftercare Plan..80
　　Case Examples..81
....82
Chapter 27: The Role of Psychodynamic Therapy in Non-clinical Settings..................83
　　Organizational Consultation..83
　　Education and Training...84
　　Community Mental Health...84
....85
Chapter 28: The Role of Psychodynamic Theory in Crisis Intervention........................86
　　Role of Psychodynamic Theory in Crisis Intervention..86
　　Working with Acute Trauma..87
　　Case Examples..87
....88
Chapter 29: Group Therapy and Psychodynamic Approaches.......................................89
　　Group Dynamics...89
　　Techniques and Considerations..90
　　Case Examples..90
　　Conclusion...91
....91
Chapter 30: Psychodynamic Therapy for Older Adults..92
　　Special Considerations for Working with Elderly Clients......................................92
　　Addressing Challenges in Aging...92
　　Case Examples..93
Chapter 31: Dual Diagnosis in Psychodynamic Therapy..94
　　Psychodynamic Understanding of Dual Diagnosis...94
　　Treatment Approaches in Psychodynamic Therapy...94
　　Case Examples..95
　　Final Thoughts..95
....95

Chapter 32: Applying Psychodynamic Principles in Real-life Cases 97
Application of Psychodynamic Principles and Techniques to Real-life Cases 97
Reflection and Discussion 98
Conclusion 99
.... 99

Chapter 33: Cultural and Societal Influences on the Development of Psychodynamic Theory 100
Influence of Culture 100
Influence of Gender 100
Influence of Society 101
Challenges and Opportunities 102
.... 102

Chapter 34: The Future of Psychodynamic Therapy 103
Emerging Trends and Innovations 103
Challenges and Opportunities 103
Unconventional Approaches and Perspectives 104
In Conclusion 104
.... 105

Chapter 35: The Importance of Continuing Education and Personal Growth as a Psychodynamic Therapist 106
The Journey of a Psychodynamic Therapist 106
The Ever-Changing Landscape of Psychology 106
The Value of Continuing Education 106
Personal Growth and Self-Reflection 107
The Role of Supervision 107
Exploring New Approaches and Techniques 107
Staying Culturally Competent 108
The Importance of Reflection and Creative Expression 108
The Impact on the Therapist-Client Relationship 108
Conclusion 108
.... 108

Chapter 36: Contributions of Other Theorists to Psychodynamic Therapy 110
Jungian, Adlerian and Object Relations Theories 110
Comparison with Freudian Theory 111
Uncommon Yet Important Concepts 111
Critiques and Controversies 112

The Future of Psychodynamic Therapy..112
Professional Development and Self-Reflection...112
Conclusion..112
....113

Chapter 37: Critiques and Controversies in Psychodynamic Therapy........114
Empirical Evidence..114
Challenges to Psychodynamic Theory and Practice.......................................115
The Role of the Therapist..115
New Directions in Psychodynamic Therapy...115
The Impact of Critiques and Controversies...116
Closing Thoughts..116
....116

Chapter 38: The Role of Therapist's Personal Experiences and Narrative in Therapy..117
The Therapist's Personal Experiences: A Source of Insight and Connection........117
The Power of Shared Experience...117
Unpacking Unconscious Biases and Countertransference............................118
The Therapeutic Narrative: Co-creating a Healing Story...............................118
Helping Clients Challenge Dominant Narratives..118
Honoring the Client's Unique Story...119
Making Meaning Out of Suffering..119
Cultivating Self-Awareness and Growth as a Therapist.................................119
Taking Care of Our Own Mental Health..120
Continued Learning and Development...120
The Beautiful Intersection of Personal and Professional..............................120
A Final Note..120
....120

Chapter 39: Personal Narratives and Personal Experience in Psychodynamic Therapy..........122
Impact of Traumatic Events on Therapists..122
Coping Strategies...122
Resilience...122

Chapter 1: Introduction to Psychodynamic Therapy

History Of Psychodynamic Therapy

Psychodynamic therapy, also known as psychoanalytic therapy, has a rich and complex history dating back to the late 19th century. It emerged as a revolutionary approach to understanding and treating mental health issues, challenging previous theories and practices that were based on surface-level symptoms. The field was initially pioneered by Sigmund Freud, often referred to as the "father of psychoanalysis," and his colleagues, who believed that mental illness was a result of unconscious conflicts and repressed emotions.

While Freud is often credited as the founder of psychodynamic therapy, it was his students and followers who further developed and refined the approach. Notable figures such as Carl Jung, Alfred Adler, and Melanie Klein expanded on Freud's theories and techniques, leading to the emergence of different schools of thought within psychodynamic therapy. These developments and diverging opinions gave rise to various offshoots, including object relations theory, self-psychology, and interpersonal psychotherapy.

Over the years, psychodynamic therapy has evolved and adapted to the changing landscape of mental health. It has influenced other therapeutic modalities such as cognitive-behavioral therapy and has contributed to our understanding of human behavior and motivation. Today, psychodynamic therapy remains a widely used and effective treatment approach for a wide range of mental health disorders.

Basic Principles And Concepts

The underlying belief of psychodynamic therapy is that individuals are influenced by unconscious factors that drive their thoughts, emotions, and behaviors. These unconscious factors, such as early childhood experiences and repressed emotions, shape how a person views the world and interacts with others.

The therapy process involves exploring these underlying factors, bringing them into the conscious mind, and working through them to promote healing and personal growth. The therapist's role is not to give advice or solutions but rather to facilitate the exploration and understanding of the client's inner world.

Another essential principle of psychodynamic therapy is the idea of transference. This refers to the client's feelings and reactions towards the therapist that are based on unconscious thoughts and emotions transferred from past relationships. Exploring transference can provide valuable insights into the client's past experiences and how they relate to their current relationships and behaviors.

The concept of resistance is another fundamental aspect of psychodynamic therapy. Resistance refers to the client's reluctance to discuss certain topics or avoid certain emotions. By exploring and working through resistance, the therapist and client can uncover underlying issues that are causing distress and work towards addressing them.

✳Comparison With Other Therapies ✳

Compared to other therapeutic modalities, psychodynamic therapy is known for its long-term and in-depth approach. Unlike cognitive-behavioral therapy, which focuses on changing specific thoughts and behaviors, psychodynamic therapy delves into the root causes of these thoughts and behaviors. It aims to create lasting changes by promoting self-awareness and insight.

Another significant difference between psychodynamic therapy and other modalities is the emphasis on the therapeutic relationship. The therapist-client relationship is seen as a crucial factor in promoting healing and change, which is why a strong bond and trust between the two are essential for successful therapy outcomes.

Furthermore, while other therapies may have a more structured and goal-oriented approach, psychodynamic therapy is more open-ended and exploratory. This allows for a deeper understanding of the client's inner world and helps build a strong foundation for lasting change.

In conclusion, psychodynamic therapy offers a unique and insightful perspective on mental health issues. Its rich history, basic principles, and unique approach set it apart from other modalities and make it a valuable tool in psychotherapy. In the following chapters, we will explore the various aspects of psychodynamic therapy in more detail and how it can be applied in clinical practice.

Chapter 2: Freud's Theory of the Unconscious

Sigmund Freud, often referred to as the father of psychoanalysis, revolutionized the field of psychology with his groundbreaking theories on the unconscious mind. While some of his ideas have been critiqued and debated over the years, his impact on the field of clinical psychology cannot be denied. In this chapter, we will explore Freud's theory of the unconscious and its role in psychodynamic therapy.

The Id

According to Freud, the mind is divided into three parts: the id, the ego, and the superego. The id is considered the most primitive and instinctual part of the mind. It is driven by our basic desires and impulses and operates on the pleasure principle, seeking immediate gratification. The id is believed to be present from birth and is responsible for our innate drives for food, water, and sex.

In psychodynamic therapy, the concept of the id helps us understand the unconscious motivations behind a client's behavior. By exploring the hidden desires and impulses that are operating in the client's id, we can gain a better understanding of their motivations and mental processes. This understanding can then guide the therapeutic process and help the client make meaningful changes in their life.

The Ego

The ego is the part of the mind that develops in early childhood and is responsible for mediating between the demands of the id and the reality of the external world. It operates on the reality principle, seeking to satisfy the id's desires in a way that is socially acceptable and realistic.

In psychodynamic therapy, the ego is seen as a crucial mediator in the therapeutic process. The therapist must work with the client to strengthen their ego, helping them develop healthier coping mechanisms and ways to satisfy their basic desires without causing harm to themselves or others. This can involve exploring defense mechanisms, such as repression or projection, that the ego uses to protect the individual from the anxiety caused by conflicting thoughts and desires.

The Superego

The superego, often referred to as the moral conscience, represents the internalized societal and parental values and beliefs that guide our behaviors. It develops during the phallic stage of psychosexual development and is believed to be influenced by the interactions with caregivers and societal norms.

In psychodynamic therapy, the superego plays a significant role in understanding the client's inner conflicts and struggles. For example, a client may have developed a harsh and critical superego due to a critical parent, which leads to feelings of shame and low self-esteem. The therapist can help the client explore and challenge these beliefs, leading to healthier self-perceptions and behaviors.

Role of Self-awareness in Psychodynamic Therapy

One of the key principles of psychodynamic therapy is the exploration of unconscious thoughts and feelings. However, in order to do so, the client must have a certain level of self-awareness. Without this self-awareness, the client may find it challenging to engage in the therapy process and make meaningful changes in their life.

As therapists, we work to help our clients develop self-awareness by providing a safe and non-judgmental space for them to explore their thoughts and emotions. Through this process, the client can gain a deeper understanding of their motivations and behaviors, as well as begin to recognize patterns in their thoughts and relationships.

Self-awareness is also crucial for developing insight, which is a key aspect of psychodynamic therapy. By gaining insight into our unconscious thoughts and feelings, we can better understand how they may be influencing our actions and behaviors. This can lead to a greater sense of self-acceptance and the ability to make positive changes in our lives.

Conclusion

In this chapter, we have explored Freud's theory of the unconscious and its role in psychodynamic therapy. The concepts of the id, ego, and superego help us understand the workings of the mind and the hidden motivations behind our thoughts and behaviors. By exploring these unconscious processes, we can gain insight and make meaningful changes in our lives. In the following chapters, we will continue to delve deeper into the world of psychodynamic therapy and how it can be applied in clinical practice.

Chapter 3: The Therapeutic Relationship

The therapeutic relationship is at the heart of psychodynamic therapy. It is the foundation upon which the entire therapeutic process is built. In this chapter, we will explore the various aspects of the therapeutic relationship, examining its importance, the concepts of transference and countertransference, and the role of boundaries in therapy.

Importance of the Therapeutic Alliance

The therapeutic alliance is the term used to describe the relationship between the therapist and the client. It is an essential aspect of psychodynamic therapy, as it provides the safe and trusting environment for the client to explore their inner world. A strong therapeutic alliance can facilitate the healing process, while a weak or strained alliance can hinder progress.

The therapist's role in creating and maintaining a strong therapeutic alliance is crucial. It is their responsibility to cultivate a supportive and empathetic stance, to be non-judgmental and open-minded, and to provide a sense of safety and trust. This allows the client to feel comfortable enough to share their deepest thoughts and emotions. One of the unique aspects of the psychodynamic approach is the emphasis on the authenticity of the relationship. In other words, the therapist is encouraged to be themselves and not hide behind a facade of professionalism. This allows for a more genuine and honest connection between the therapist and the client.

The therapeutic alliance also plays a role in the client's motivation and willingness to engage in therapy. A positive relationship can increase the client's commitment and motivation to work through challenging feelings and experiences, maintaining a sense of hope and belief in the therapy process.

Transference and Countertransference

Transference and countertransference are two concepts that are central to psychodynamic therapy. Transference occurs when the client projects feelings and attitudes towards significant figures in their lives onto the therapist. This can include positive feelings such as love and admiration, or negative feelings such as anger and resentment.

On the other hand, countertransference is the therapist's emotional reaction to the client, which is influenced by their personal history and experiences. It is essential for the therapist to be aware of their countertransference reactions, as they can provide valuable insights into the client's internal dynamics and transference patterns.

Both transference and countertransference can be beneficial in therapy if they are recognized and understood. By acknowledging and exploring these dynamics within the therapeutic relationship, the therapist and client can gain a deeper understanding of the client's underlying issues and work through them in a safe and controlled environment.

Boundaries in Therapy

Boundaries refer to the limits and expectations of the therapist-client relationship. They are necessary to maintain a professional and ethical therapeutic environment and to avoid enmeshment or exploitation.

In psychodynamic therapy, the concept of boundaries is crucial, as the therapeutic relationship itself can sometimes provoke intense and complicated feelings in the client. By establishing clear and consistent boundaries, the therapist can create a safe and stable space for the client to explore their thoughts and emotions.

At the same time, boundaries can also be flexible and adapt to the client's needs. For example, in moments where the client may need more support and closeness, the therapist may adjust the boundaries to provide a more nurturing and empathetic stance. However, these adjustments should always be made with careful consideration to maintain the overall integrity of the therapeutic relationship.

In conclusion, the therapeutic relationship is a dynamic and essential aspect of psychodynamic therapy. It is built upon the strong foundation of the therapeutic alliance, open communication, and the awareness of transference and countertransference dynamics. Through the therapist's cultivation of a supportive and safe environment, the client can explore their inner world and work towards healing and growth. Maintaining clear boundaries also ensures the ethical and professional integrity of the therapeutic relationship.

Chapter 4: Techniques in Psychodynamic Therapy

Free Association

Freud is often credited with the development of free association, a technique that is still widely used in psychodynamic therapy today. Free association involves encouraging the client to freely share thoughts, feelings, and memories without censorship or judgment. This allows for the exploration and examination of unconscious material that may be contributing to current issues and symptoms.

As therapists, we are taught to listen for patterns and associations in our clients' free associations. These can often reveal underlying conflicts or struggles that the conscious mind may be unaware of. By exploring these associations, clients can gain insight and understanding into their motivations and behaviors.

Free association can also be a powerful tool for uncovering repressed memories or traumas. Through consistent and open free association, clients may be able to access and process these suppressed emotions. This can be a cathartic and healing experience, leading to a decrease in symptoms and an increase in self-awareness.

Dream Analysis

Dreams have long been a source of fascination and mystery, and in psychodynamic therapy, they hold significant value in the exploration of the unconscious. Dream analysis involves unpacking the symbolism and meaning behind a client's dreams in order to gain insight into their inner conflicts and desires. In psychodynamic theory, dreams are seen as a manifestation of the unconscious, containing repressed or hidden emotions and thoughts. By exploring the content and themes of dreams, clients can gain a better understanding of their unconscious processes and conflicts.

Dream analysis can also be used as a therapeutic technique to help clients work through current problems or issues. By exploring their dreams, clients may uncover new perspectives or solutions to their struggles. Dreams can also provide a safe space for clients to process and express difficult emotions or experiences.

Projective Tests

Projective tests are a set of guided assessments designed to reveal a client's underlying thoughts, feelings, and conflicts. These tests are often used in psychodynamic therapy to help clients gain insight into their unconscious processes.

One of the most well-known projective tests is the Rorschach Inkblot test, where clients are asked to describe what they see in a series of inkblots. Through their responses, the therapist can gather information about the client's personality, emotions, and perceptions. Another commonly used projective test is the Thematic Apperception Test (TAT), where clients are shown a series of ambiguous pictures and asked to create a story about each one. The stories can reveal underlying thoughts and motivations that the client may not be aware of. Projective tests can be a powerful tool for uncovering unconscious material and providing a deeper understanding of a client's struggles. However, they should be used in conjunction with other assessment and therapeutic techniques for a comprehensive understanding of the client.

Incorporating Techniques into Therapy

While these three techniques - free association, dream analysis, and projective tests - are all commonly used in psychodynamic therapy, it is important to note that they are not the focus of therapy. Instead, they are tools that can be used to help clients gain insight and understanding into their unconscious processes.

Additionally, it is essential for therapists to approach these techniques with caution and sensitivity. Clients may have varying levels of comfort and readiness to explore their unconscious, and pushing too hard or too soon can be counterproductive. A strong therapeutic relationship and trust between therapist and client is crucial for the success of these techniques.

Incorporating these techniques into therapy requires a balance of structure and flexibility. While free association allows for a client-led exploration, dream analysis and projective tests provide some structure and guidance. It is up to the therapist to navigate these techniques in a way that best suits the individual needs and goals of each client.

In Conclusion

Techniques in psychodynamic therapy, such as free association, dream analysis, and projective tests, are powerful tools that can help clients gain insight, understanding, and healing. Through these techniques, therapists and clients can explore the hidden depths of the unconscious, uncovering the root causes of issues and building a stronger sense of self-awareness.

As with all aspects of psychodynamic therapy, the focus remains on the therapeutic relationship and the client's growth and development. These techniques are meant to be utilized with care and consideration, in collaboration with the client, for the best possible outcomes.

Chapter 5: Understanding Psychodynamic Assessment

In the field of clinical psychology, assessments are vital in determining the most appropriate treatment plan for clients. While there are many different types of assessments, the Psychodynamic Diagnostic Manual (PDM) sets itself apart through its focus on understanding the individual's internal world and the underlying psychological patterns that contribute to their current state. In this chapter, we will explore the process of developing a psychodynamic formulation, conducting a psychodynamic assessment, and using case conceptualization to understand the complexities of the individual's psyche.

Psychodynamic Diagnostic Manual

The Psychodynamic Diagnostic Manual (PDM) was developed to guide clinicians in psychodynamic assessment and diagnosis. Instead of focusing solely on surface symptoms, the manual looks at the underlying state of the unconscious mind and how it influences the person's behavior and relationships. This approach is rooted in the psychodynamic theory, which emphasizes the importance of early childhood experiences and the role of unconscious conflicts in shaping one's personality and behavior.

One of the unique aspects of the PDM is its focus on the individual's subjective experience and the therapist's countertransference as a valid source of information. This means that the therapist is encouraged to explore their own emotional reactions and internal processes as they interact with the client. By doing so, the therapist gains a deeper understanding of the individual's inner world, allowing for a more accurate assessment and formulation.

Developing a Psychodynamic Formulation

A psychodynamic formulation is a detailed understanding of the individual's personality, conflicts, and patterns of behavior, informed by psychodynamic theory and concepts. It is an ongoing process that involves gathering and integrating information from various sources, including the individual's presenting symptoms, history, and interactions with the therapist.

To develop a psychodynamic formulation, the therapist must have a deep understanding of the individual's unconscious processes, such as defense mechanisms, internalized objects, and early childhood experiences. This requires the therapist to use their knowledge of psychodynamic theory, as well as their intuition and empathy, to carefully explore and interpret the individual's experiences and behavior.

The formulation can be thought of as a map of the individual's inner world, guiding the treatment and helping the therapist understand the client's emotions, motivations, and defenses. By having a comprehensive understanding of the individual, the formulation allows for a more tailored and effective treatment approach.

Case Conceptualization

Case conceptualization is the process of using the formulation to understand the complexity of the individual's psychological makeup and how it relates to their current difficulties. It involves linking the individual's past experiences and unconscious conflicts to their current symptoms and behaviors, providing a deeper understanding of their unique struggles.

One essential aspect of case conceptualization is the focus on the therapeutic relationship. As the therapist and client interact, transference and countertransference dynamics arise, providing valuable insight into the individual's internal world. By exploring the unconscious meanings of these dynamics, the therapist gains a deeper understanding of the individual's struggles and can use this information to guide the treatment.

It is important to note that case conceptualization is an ongoing and collaborative process between the therapist and the client. As the individual gains insight into their own experiences and internal processes, they become active participants in the case conceptualization. This collaboration fosters a therapeutic alliance, allowing for more effective treatment.

Conclusion

In conclusion, psychodynamic assessment and case conceptualization are crucial components in understanding and treating individuals through the psychodynamic lens. By using the PDM, developing a psychodynamic formulation, and engaging in case conceptualization, therapists can gain a deeper understanding of their clients' inner world and provide more tailored and effective treatment. As a continuous and collaborative process, it allows for a more intimate and meaningful therapeutic relationship, leading to lasting change and growth.

Chapter 6: Childhood and Developmental Issues

Freud's Psychosexual Stages

When discussing psychodynamic therapy, it is impossible to overlook the contributions of Sigmund Freud and his theories on psychosexual development. According to Freud, our experiences in childhood shape our personality and behavior as adults. He proposed that there are five stages of psychosexual development, each associated with different erogenous zones and conflicts that must be successfully resolved for healthy development. These stages include the oral, anal, phallic, latent, and genital stages.

The oral stage, which occurs in the first 18 months of life, is centered around the mouth and feeding. During this stage, infants experience pleasure and gratification through sucking and biting. If a child does not receive enough oral stimulation, they may develop oral fixations such as excessive talking or smoking as adults. On the other hand, if a child is overstimulated in this stage, they may develop oral aggressive behaviors and become demanding, manipulative, and aggressive in their relationships.

The anal stage occurs between 18 months and 3 years of age and centers around toilet training. This stage is crucial in developing a sense of control and autonomy. If a child is too harshly disciplined during this stage, they may become overly rigid and controlled as adults. Alternatively, if a child is not properly toilet trained, they may develop messiness and disorganization in their adult life.

The phallic stage, between 3 and 6 years of age, is when children become aware of their gender and sexual differences. During this stage, they may develop unconscious desires for the opposite-sex parent and experience jealousy towards the same-sex parent. If these desires are not successfully resolved, they may lead to issues with identity, relationships, and ultimately, mental health.

The latency stage, which occurs from 6 years to puberty, is a period of relative calm in psychosexual development. Children during this stage tend to focus on developing social and cognitive skills. However, unresolved conflicts from previous stages may still manifest in the form of anxiety, phobias, or other psychological disturbances.

Finally, the genital stage, which begins at puberty, marks the return of sexual desires and urges. If everything goes well in previous stages, individuals will have developed a healthy sense of self and the ability to form satisfying relationships. However, if conflicts from previous stages remain unresolved, they may continue to impact our relationships and functioning as adults.

Psychodynamic Understanding of Attachment

The concept of attachment is another essential aspect of psychodynamic therapy. According to attachment theory, developed by John Bowlby and further expanded by Mary Ainsworth, our early attachment experiences with our caregivers shape our relationships and emotional regulation as adults. Bowlby proposed that a secure attachment with a primary caregiver is crucial for healthy development, and any disruptions in this attachment may lead to difficulties in later relationships. Attachment styles, which are formed based on early attachment experiences, influence how individuals interact with others and their perceptions of themselves. A secure attachment style enables individuals to form healthy relationships, while insecure attachment styles, such as anxious or avoidant, may limit their ability to form and maintain meaningful connections.

In psychodynamic therapy, understanding attachment styles and patterns is essential for addressing interpersonal issues and helping clients develop more secure and satisfying relationships. Through exploring early attachment experiences and dynamics, individuals can gain insight into how these experiences may influence their current relationships and work towards resolving any conflicts and developing more secure attachment patterns.

Impact of Childhood Experiences on Adult Functioning

As we have seen, both Freud's theories on psychosexual development and attachment theory emphasize the importance of childhood experiences in shaping our adult selves. However, psychodynamic therapy goes beyond these theories and acknowledges that all childhood experiences, both positive and negative, may impact our development and functioning as adults.

Unresolved conflicts and traumas from childhood may manifest in various ways, such as low self-esteem, relationship difficulties, anxiety, depression, or other mental health issues. In psychodynamic therapy, individuals are encouraged to explore and process these experiences in a safe and supportive environment. By gaining insight into these experiences and their impact, individuals can work towards resolving any conflicts and developing healthier coping mechanisms.

It is also worth noting that positive childhood experiences, such as secure attachments and healthy emotional expression, can have a significant impact on our mental health and wellbeing. In addition, our childhood experiences can shape our expectations and perceptions of the world, influencing our choices and behavior as adults.

In conclusion, childhood and developmental issues are central to psychodynamic therapy. By understanding how our early experiences shape our personality, relationships, and functioning as adults, we can gain insight into our struggles and work towards healing and personal growth. Through exploring and processing childhood experiences, individuals can develop a deeper understanding of themselves and develop healthier coping mechanisms for a more fulfilling life.

Chapter 7: Defense Mechanisms

Types of Defense Mechanisms

Defense mechanisms are unconscious psychological strategies that individuals use to cope with stress, anxiety, and other uncomfortable emotions. They are meant to protect the individual from the distressing thoughts and feelings that may arise from conflicts and unresolved issues. Sigmund Freud, the father of psychoanalytic theory, first identified defense mechanisms and their role in protection against anxiety.

There are various types of defense mechanisms, and they can be categorized into different groups based on their function. Some of the most common types include denial, projection, repression, displacement, rationalization, and sublimation. Each defense mechanism serves a different purpose, and understanding them can help individuals gain insight into their own behavior and thought patterns.

Role in Coping with Stress

Defense mechanisms play a crucial role in helping individuals cope with stressful situations and emotions. They serve as a protective barrier and allow individuals to maintain their emotional well-being, even in the face of difficult circumstances. When faced with a stressful event or overwhelming emotions, the mind may unconsciously utilize one or more defense mechanisms to avoid confronting the situation directly. This can provide temporary relief and allow the individual to function without being overwhelmed by their emotions.

However, it is essential to note that relying too heavily on defense mechanisms can be harmful in the long run. While they may provide temporary relief, they do not address the underlying issues that are causing stress or anxiety. In fact, defense mechanisms can often create barriers to personal growth and hinder the individual's ability to cope with future challenges effectively.

Recognizing and Working with Defense Mechanisms in Therapy

As a therapist, it is crucial to have an understanding of defense mechanisms and their role in coping with stress. By recognizing these defense mechanisms in our clients, we can help them gain insight into their behaviors and thought patterns. This awareness allows individuals to explore and address the underlying issues that are causing their distress.

An essential aspect of working with defense mechanisms in therapy is creating a safe and non-judgmental space for clients to explore their emotions and behaviors. By fostering a trusting therapeutic relationship, clients can feel comfortable sharing their thoughts and feelings, including those that may be protected by defense mechanisms.

Working with defense mechanisms in therapy also involves helping clients recognize when these mechanisms are being used and how they may be hindering their personal growth. This can be a challenging process, as individuals may have developed these defenses as a means of survival. But with patience and understanding, clients can learn to recognize and challenge their defense mechanisms, allowing for more authentic and meaningful growth.

Furthermore, as a therapist, it is essential to explore alternative coping strategies and help clients develop healthier ways of managing stress and emotions. This may involve utilizing techniques such as mindfulness, relaxation techniques, or communication skills to address conflicts and issues directly.

In conclusion, defense mechanisms are complex and adaptive strategies that individuals use to cope with stress and difficult emotions. While they may serve as a protective barrier, they can also hinder personal growth and prevent individuals from addressing underlying issues. As therapists, it is crucial to recognize and work with defense mechanisms to help our clients gain insight and develop healthier coping strategies. By creating a non-judgmental and supportive therapeutic environment, we can help clients move towards a more fulfilling and authentic life.

Chapter 8: Addressing Resistance in Psychodynamic Therapy

Understanding Resistance

Psychodynamic therapy is a therapy approach that focuses on exploring unconscious thoughts and emotions in order to understand and treat psychological issues. It is a powerful and effective approach, but it is not without its challenges. One of the most common challenges in psychodynamic therapy is client resistance.

Resistance can be defined as any form of opposition or unwillingness to engage in the therapeutic process. It can manifest in various ways, such as missed appointments, lack of participation in therapy sessions, or being guarded and defensive in one's communication. Resistance is often seen as a barrier to progress in therapy, as it can hinder the exploration of important unconscious material.

In psychodynamic therapy, resistance is seen as a natural and expected response to the exploration of unconscious material. It is seen as a protective mechanism that aims to keep unconscious thoughts and feelings hidden from conscious awareness. Therefore, understanding and addressing resistance is an essential part of the psychodynamic therapy process.

Reasons for Resistance

There are many reasons why clients may resist psychodynamic therapy. One of the most common reasons is fear. Clients may fear what they will uncover in therapy, as it can be uncomfortable and even painful to face deep-seated issues. This fear can lead to avoidance and resistance to therapy. Additionally, clients may also fear the therapist's interpretation and judgment of their unconscious material.

Another reason for resistance is lack of trust. Clients may struggle to trust the therapist or the therapeutic process, which can lead to resistance. This lack of trust may stem from past negative experiences with therapy or other relationships. Clients may also feel hesitant to open up and be vulnerable with someone they do not know well.

Resistance may also occur when there is a discrepancy between the therapist's and client's goals for therapy. Clients may resist exploring certain issues or aspects of their personality if they do not align with their personal goals. Similarly, if the client does not feel heard or understood by the therapist, they may resist engaging in the therapeutic process.

Strategies for Addressing Resistance

Addressing resistance in psychodynamic therapy requires a gentle and empathetic approach. It is essential for the therapist to create a safe and trusting therapeutic relationship to reduce resistance. This can be done by actively listening to the client, being non-judgmental, and providing support and validation for the client's experiences.

It is also crucial for the therapist to help clients understand the purpose of resistance. By educating clients on the role of resistance in therapy, they may feel less threatened and more willing to engage in the process. The therapist may also explore the underlying fears or concerns that are leading to resistance and help the client address them.

Another effective strategy for addressing resistance is to work collaboratively with the client and involve them in the therapeutic process. This can help the client feel more in control of their therapy and reduce feelings of resistance. The therapist may also use various techniques, such as dream interpretation or free association, to bypass the client's conscious defenses and gain access to their unconscious material.

Finally, it is important for the therapist to be aware of their own countertransference and how it may contribute to resistance in therapy. Countertransference refers to the therapist's unconscious reactions to the client, which may stem from their own unresolved issues. By working through their own countertransference, therapists can better understand and address the client's resistance.

Conclusion

Resistance is a natural and expected part of the psychodynamic therapy process. However, by understanding the reasons for resistance and using effective strategies for addressing it, therapists can help clients overcome their resistance and make meaningful progress in therapy. It is important for therapists to maintain a compassionate and non-judgmental stance towards their clients' resistance, as it is often a sign of deeper underlying issues that need to be explored. By working through resistance, clients can gain a better understanding of themselves and make meaningful changes in their lives.

Chapter 9: Understanding and Treating Depression, Bipolar Disorder and Psychodynamic Therapy

Understanding and Treating Depression

Depression is a complex and multifaceted mental health disorder that affects millions of people worldwide. It is not simply feeling sad or blue, but a pervasive and persistent feeling of hopelessness, worthlessness, and sadness. While there is no one cause of depression, factors such as genetics, environmental stressors, and brain chemistry imbalances are all considered to contribute to its development. One of the key aspects in understanding depression is recognizing its two distinct types: major depressive disorder (MDD) and persistent depressive disorder (PDD). MDD is characterized by recurrent episodes of intense and debilitating depression, while PDD is characterized by a longer-lasting but less severe form of depression. Both types can severely impact an individual's daily functioning, relationships, and overall quality of life. In psychodynamic therapy, depression is often seen as a manifestation of unresolved conflicts and unconscious defense mechanisms. The therapy focuses on exploring a person's past experiences, early attachment patterns, and interpersonal relationships to uncover the underlying causes of their depression. By bringing these unconscious thoughts and feelings into awareness, the therapist and client can work together to create meaningful insights and develop healthier coping mechanisms.

Bipolar Disorder and Psychodynamic Therapy

Bipolar disorder is a mood disorder that is marked by extreme shifts in mood, energy, and activity levels. It is often characterized by periods of intense mania and depression, which can significantly affect a person's relationships, work, and daily functioning. While the causes of bipolar disorder are not fully understood, it is believed to be linked to a combination of genetic, biological, and environmental factors.

For individuals with bipolar disorder, psychodynamic therapy can be an effective approach in managing symptoms and improving overall functioning. The therapy helps individuals gain a better understanding of their emotions and how they are linked to their past experiences and relationships. It also provides a safe and supportive space to explore their thoughts and feelings related to their manic and depressive episodes. By recognizing and addressing underlying conflicts and issues, individuals can learn new ways to regulate their moods and cope with their symptoms.

Case Examples

To illustrate the effectiveness of psychodynamic therapy in treating depression and bipolar disorder, let us consider the case of Sarah. Sarah was a 32-year-old woman who had been struggling with depression since her teenage years. She had been diagnosed with major depressive disorder and had been on and off medication for years. Despite trying various forms of therapy, Sarah had not found relief from her symptoms and was getting increasingly frustrated. In psychodynamic therapy, Sarah was able to explore the root causes of her depression, which she had never fully addressed before. She had a history of traumatic experiences in her childhood, and through therapy, she was able to process and make sense of those experiences. Additionally, Sarah's therapist helped her identify and challenge her self-defeating thoughts and beliefs that perpetuated her depression.

As a result of her therapy, Sarah learned to understand and regulate her emotions, rebuild her self-esteem, and make healthier choices in her relationships and daily life. She also became more aware of her triggers and developed coping strategies to manage her depressive episodes. While she still experienced periods of low mood, they were now more manageable, and she had gained a deeper understanding of herself and her past.

Another example is the case of Michael, a 26-year-old man with bipolar disorder. Michael had been struggling with fluctuating moods and energy levels since adolescence, and it had severely impacted his relationships and work. He had a history of strained relationships with his family and had never fully come to terms with his diagnosis. In psychodynamic therapy, Michael was able to explore his past experiences and relationships, which had shaped his view of himself and his illness. He also learned to regulate his emotions and identify the early signs of his manic and depressive episodes. With the support of his therapist, Michael was able to improve his self-esteem and develop healthier ways of relating to others. He also learned to accept his diagnosis and manage his symptoms more effectively.

Through these case studies, we can see how psychodynamic therapy can be an effective approach in understanding and treating depression and bipolar disorder. By delving into the unconscious factors, exploring past experiences, and developing a new sense of self, individuals can find relief from their symptoms and lead more fulfilling lives.

In conclusion, depression and bipolar disorder are complex and debilitating disorders that require a comprehensive approach in treatment. Psychodynamic therapy offers a unique and effective way of understanding and addressing these conditions by exploring the unconscious, past experiences, and relationships. By uncovering and working through underlying issues, individuals can gain a deeper understanding of themselves and learn to manage their symptoms more effectively.

Chapter 10: Understanding and Treating Generalized Anxiety Disorder, Panic Disorder, OCD, and Psychodynamic Therapy

Understanding and Treating GAD

Generalized Anxiety Disorder (GAD) can often be misunderstood and overlooked in the realm of mental health. It is a common disorder that affects millions of people worldwide, yet it is still shrouded in misconceptions and stigmas. GAD is characterized by chronic and excessive worry and anxiety about various aspects of life, such as work, relationships, finances, and health. These worries are often constant and overwhelming, making it difficult for those with GAD to fully enjoy and engage in daily activities.

One of the most important things to understand about GAD is that it is not something that an individual can simply "snap out of." It is a complex disorder that involves a combination of biological, psychological, and environmental factors. There is no single cause for GAD, and it can manifest differently in each individual. However, research suggests that individuals with GAD often have an overactive amygdala, the part of the brain responsible for processing emotions and fear. This can lead to heightened sensitivity to potential threats, causing persistent worry and fear.

While there is no known cure for GAD, psychodynamic therapy has shown to be particularly effective in treating this disorder. This type of therapy focuses on exploring and understanding the underlying causes and conflicts that contribute to an individual's symptoms. By delving into unconscious thoughts and emotions, individuals with GAD can gain insight into their anxiety and learn ways to manage and cope with it.

Understanding and Treating Panic Disorder

Panic Disorder is a debilitating anxiety disorder characterized by sudden and recurrent panic attacks. These attacks can be triggered by a specific situation or can occur unexpectedly, leading to intense physical and emotional experiences. Panic attacks can include symptoms such as heart palpitations, shortness of breath, dizziness, and a sense of dread or impending doom. These symptoms can be so severe that individuals may feel like they are having a heart attack, causing them to seek emergency medical help.

Much like GAD, Panic Disorder has no single cause, but it is believed to be a combination of biological, environmental, and psychological factors. One common factor found in individuals with Panic Disorder is a history of trauma or a significant life event, such as a loss of a loved one or a difficult divorce. The experience of intense emotions during these events can cause individuals to develop an anxious mindset, making them more susceptible to panic attacks later on.

Psychodynamic therapy can be especially helpful in treating Panic Disorder by addressing the underlying unresolved conflicts and emotions from past experiences. By working through those experiences, individuals with Panic Disorder can learn to manage and lessen the intensity of panic attacks. Therapy can also help individuals develop coping strategies and self-soothing techniques to use during a panic attack, reducing the severity of symptoms.

Understanding and Treating OCD

Obsessive-Compulsive Disorder (OCD) is a disorder that is characterized by intrusive and unwanted thoughts (obsessions) and repetitive behaviors or mental acts (compulsions). These obsessions and compulsions can consume a significant amount of an individual's time and interfere with their daily life and relationships. Common obsessions may include fear of contamination, fear of harm to oneself or others, or fear of making a mistake. Compulsions often involve repetitive behaviors such as handwashing, checking, or counting. There is no clear cause of OCD, but research suggests that it may be due to a combination of genetic, biological, and environmental factors. Some studies have also shown that individuals with OCD may have differences in brain structure and function, specifically in areas responsible for decision-making and emotional processing.

Psychodynamic therapy can be effective in treating OCD by helping individuals explore the root causes of their obsessions and compulsions. By understanding the underlying emotions and conflicts related to these thoughts and behaviors, individuals can learn to break free from the cycle of obsessions and compulsions. Therapy can also help individuals develop healthier coping strategies to manage their anxiety and reduce the frequency and intensity of their symptoms.

Psychodynamic Therapy and Case Examples

An example of how psychodynamic therapy can be effective in treating GAD is the case of Sarah. Sarah presented to therapy with symptoms of chronic worry and anxiety, particularly about her relationships and her health. Through exploring her childhood experiences with her parents as well as her current relationships, Sarah came to understand how her anxiety was rooted in unresolved feelings of abandonment and fear of rejection. As she worked through her feelings in therapy, Sarah was able to better manage her anxiety and build healthier relationships.

In the case of John, who has Panic Disorder, psychodynamic therapy helped him identify the underlying cause of his panic attacks - his fear of losing control. Through exploring his past experiences and engaging in a deeper understanding of himself, John was able to gain insight into the root of his fear. With the help of his therapist, he learned to cope with his feelings of fear and assert control over his panic attacks.

Finally, in the case of OCD, psychodynamic therapy has been shown to help individuals like Alex, who had a fear of contamination. Alex's compulsive hand washing and cleaning were rooted in his childhood experiences with his strict and perfectionistic parents. Through therapy, Alex was able to understand how his childhood experiences influenced his current behaviors and learned to address his feelings of inadequacy and self-criticism.

In conclusion, psychodynamic therapy can be a valuable tool in treating GAD, Panic Disorder, and OCD. By exploring and understanding the underlying emotions and conflicts that contribute to these disorders, individuals can gain insight into their symptoms and develop healthier coping strategies. Psychodynamic therapy offers a holistic approach to treatment, addressing the individual as a whole and not just their symptoms, leading to long-term healing and well-being.

Chapter 11: Personality Disorders in Psychodynamic Therapy

Types of Personality Disorders

Personality disorders are complex and persistent patterns of thoughts, feelings, and behaviors that deviate from cultural expectations and cause significant distress or impairment. In the fifth edition of the Diagnostic and Statistical Manual of Mental Disorders (DSM-5), there are ten defined personality disorders, categorized into three clusters: Cluster A (odd or eccentric), Cluster B (dramatic, emotional, or erratic), and Cluster C (anxious or fearful). Each type of personality disorder presents unique challenges in therapeutic work and requires specific treatment approaches.

Cluster A personality disorders include paranoid, schizoid, and schizotypal personality disorders. These individuals may struggle with social interactions, have odd beliefs or behaviors, and lack close relationships. Cluster B personality disorders include antisocial, borderline, histrionic, and narcissistic personality disorders. Individuals with these disorders may have difficulty regulating emotions, display impulsive behaviors, and have unstable relationships. Cluster C personality disorders include avoidant, dependent, and obsessive-compulsive personality disorders. These individuals often have difficulty with attachment and display inflexible behaviors or perfectionistic tendencies.

Psychodynamic Understanding and Treatment

In psychodynamic therapy, the focus is on the unconscious processes that influence a person's thoughts, feelings, and behaviors. Therefore, understanding the inner workings of the personality is essential when treating personality disorders. Psychodynamic theorists believe that early childhood experiences and unresolved conflicts contribute significantly to the development of personality disorders.

Personality disorders are deeply ingrained patterns that are hard to change, and the treatment process may take a longer time compared to treating other clinical conditions. Psychodynamic therapy aims to uncover and work through early childhood traumas, maladaptive defense mechanisms, and repeated patterns of behavior that contribute to the maintenance of personality disorders. The therapeutic relationship is a crucial factor in psychodynamic therapy, as it allows individuals to transfer patterns of relating from their past to the therapist, creating an opportunity for change.

In the treatment of personality disorders, the therapist must maintain a non-authoritative stance, collaborating with the client in exploring their feelings and childhood experiences. The therapist also needs to focus on developing insight, fostering emotional expression, and repairing the fragmented self. The use of techniques such as dream interpretation, free association, and transference analysis can help individuals gain insight into their underlying motivations and unresolved conflicts. Therapists may also work on helping the client develop healthier coping mechanisms and more adaptive ways of relating to others.

Case Examples

Case Example 1:

Jane was diagnosed with borderline personality disorder and had a history of unstable relationships and self-harming behaviors. In therapy, Jane's therapist used psychodynamic techniques to help her explore her childhood experiences and the origins of her intense emotions and impulsive behaviors. Through the therapeutic relationship, Jane was able to develop a secure attachment with her therapist, leading to increased trust and the ability to process traumatic events from her past. By gaining insight into her unresolved conflicts and underlying motivations, Jane was able to develop healthier coping mechanisms and build more stable and fulfilling relationships.

Case Example 2:

John was diagnosed with avoidant personality disorder and had a long-standing fear of social interactions and rejection. Through psychodynamic therapy, John's therapist helped him examine his early childhood experiences of neglect and mistreatment that contributed to his fear of rejection. John and his therapist worked together to challenge his negative self-perceptions and build self-esteem. As the therapy progressed, John was able to overcome his avoidant behaviors and develop more meaningful connections with others.

Conclusion

Personality disorders can significantly impact an individual's life, causing distress and difficulties in relationships and functioning. However, with the specialized understanding and treatment techniques of psychodynamic therapy, individuals with personality disorders can gain insight and work towards change in a safe therapeutic setting. By addressing underlying conflicts, developing insight, and enhancing coping mechanisms, individuals with personality disorders can experience growth and improve their quality of life. The importance of the therapeutic relationship in this process cannot be overstated, as it offers a supportive and reparative experience that can lead to lasting change.

Chapter 12: Understanding Trauma

Trauma is a significant aspect of the human experience that impacts individuals in profound ways. It can arise from a variety of sources, including violent events, accidents, natural disasters, and even ongoing emotional abuse. Traumatic experiences can leave deep scars, causing individuals to feel overwhelmed, helpless, and disconnected from the world around them. It is essential for therapists to have a comprehensive understanding of trauma and its effects so they can effectively support individuals on their journey towards healing and recovery.

Understanding Trauma

Trauma is not a one-size-fits-all experience, where individuals have the same reactions and responses to events. It is a complex and highly individualized experience, influenced by several factors, including one's unique psychological makeup, past experiences, and cultural background. Trauma can manifest in various ways, such as acute stress disorder, post-traumatic stress disorder (PTSD), and complex trauma.

When individuals are exposed to a traumatic event, their brains undergo changes in functioning. The amygdala, often referred to as the "fear center" of the brain, becomes hyperactive, leading to heightened fear and anxiety responses. The prefrontal cortex, responsible for logical reasoning, memory, and planning, may also be affected, making it challenging to process and cope with the traumatic event.

Importance of Processing Traumatic Memories

Processing and integrating traumatic memories is a crucial aspect of trauma therapy. Many individuals may try to avoid recalling or thinking about the traumatic event, which can lead to avoidance and numbing as a coping mechanism. However, avoiding or suppressing traumatic memories can cause them to resurface in later life, leading to a profound impact on an individual's mental and emotional well-being.

Therapists must create a safe and supportive environment where individuals can share their experiences and process their traumatic memories. By doing so, therapists can help individuals make sense of their trauma and move towards integrating it into their overall life narrative. This process can be challenging and may involve exploring and addressing difficult emotions and thoughts. Still, it is a necessary step towards healing and recovery.

Techniques for Working with Traumatic Reactions

Psychodynamic therapy offers a range of techniques to support individuals in processing and working through their traumatic reactions. One such technique is psychoanalysis, where the therapist helps individuals explore and gain insight into their unconscious processes, unresolved conflicts, and repressed emotions related to the trauma. By understanding the underlying dynamics at play, individuals can gain a deeper understanding of their reactions and develop healthier coping mechanisms. Another technique is trauma-focused cognitive-behavioral therapy (TF-CBT), which combines cognitive-behavioral therapy (CBT) with trauma-focused interventions. This modality helps individuals identify and challenge negative thoughts and beliefs related to the trauma and learn practical skills to manage their reactions and emotions. As trauma can often disrupt an individual's sense of safety and trust in others, building a therapeutic alliance is crucial in supporting individuals' healing process.

In recent years, research has also shown the effectiveness of psychodynamic approaches, such as eye movement desensitization and reprocessing (EMDR) and somatic experiencing, in treating trauma. These techniques aim to help individuals access and process their traumatic memories by focusing on the mind-body connection.

In conclusion, working with trauma requires therapists to have a thorough understanding of the complexities and impact of trauma on individuals. By creating a safe and supportive space and utilizing a variety of techniques, therapists can help individuals process and integrate their traumatic memories, leading towards healing and transformation.

Chapter 13: The Art of Healing Relationships

Relationships are at the very core of human existence. From the moment we are born, we form bonds and connections with others. These relationships play a fundamental role in shaping our identities and impacting our mental health. However, relationships can also be a source of great pain and conflict. In this chapter, we will explore the complexities of relationships and how psychodynamic therapy can help heal and improve them.

Understanding and Treating Relationship Issues

Relationship issues can present in various forms, from difficulties in communication and intimacy to ongoing conflicts and power imbalances. These issues often stem from unaddressed emotional wounds and traumas from the past, which can manifest in the dynamics of current relationships. Psychodynamic therapy offers a unique approach to understanding and treating relationship issues by exploring the roots of these struggles.

One key element of psychodynamic therapy is the idea of the unconscious. This refers to the parts of our mind that we are not fully aware of but still greatly influence our thoughts, feelings, and behaviors. In the context of relationships, the unconscious holds onto past experiences and emotions, which can shape our present interactions with others. For example, a person who has experienced abandonment in their childhood may struggle with intense fears of rejection and have difficulty forming trusting relationships.

In psychodynamic therapy, the therapist works collaboratively with the client to explore their underlying, unconscious conflicts and traumas. By shedding light on these hidden dynamics, clients can gain a better understanding of how their past experiences may be impacting their present relationships. This awareness can lead to healing and transformation, ultimately improving the quality of their relationships.

Attachment Styles and Conflict Resolution

An important aspect of relationships is attachment styles. Attachment theory suggests that our early relationships with primary caregivers shape our attachment styles, which in turn impact our relationships in adulthood. There are four main attachment styles: secure, anxious-preoccupied, dismissive-avoidant, and fearful-avoidant. Clients often come to therapy with attachment issues, and their attachment styles can greatly influence their relationships.

In psychodynamic therapy, therapists pay attention to attachment dynamics and help clients understand how their attachment styles may be contributing to their relationship difficulties. For example, someone with a dismissive-avoidant attachment style may struggle with emotional intimacy and have a tendency to withdraw from their partner during times of conflict. By exploring the roots of attachment styles, clients can gain insight into their patterns and work towards developing more secure attachments in their relationships.

Conflict resolution is another crucial aspect of relationships that can greatly benefit from psychodynamic therapy. Conflict is a natural and inevitable part of any relationship, but it is how we handle it that can make or break a relationship. In psychodynamic therapy, clients can explore their conflict patterns and learn effective communication skills to address and resolve conflicts in a healthy manner. This can create a more fulfilling and harmonious relationship with others.

Case Examples

To better understand the application of psychodynamic therapy in healing relationships, let us take a look at two case examples.

Case 1: Jane is a 32-year-old woman struggling with feelings of insecurity and anxiety in her marriage. She often feels rejected and not good enough for her husband, who she perceives as emotionally distant. In therapy, Jane reveals that her father was emotionally unavailable and constantly criticized her during her childhood. She also experienced a traumatic event in her adulthood that further reinforced her belief that she is unworthy of love. Through psychodynamic therapy, Jane begins to make connections between her past experiences and her current relationship issues. With this newfound awareness, she can work on healing her wounds and develop healthier ways of communicating with her husband.

Case 2: John is a 45-year-old man who is struggling with anger issues and frequent conflicts with his coworkers. In therapy, he reveals that he had a tumultuous relationship with his mother, who would often get angry at him for minor things. John learned to suppress his feelings and developed a habit of lashing out when frustrated or overwhelmed. Through psychodynamic therapy, he learns to identify his triggers and develop healthier coping mechanisms to manage his anger. As a result, his relationships with his coworkers improve, and he feels more in control of his emotions.

These cases demonstrate the power of psychodynamic therapy in healing relationships by exploring the unconscious and addressing underlying issues. By understanding and addressing these issues, clients can experience positive changes in their relationships and their overall well-being.

In Conclusion

Relationships are complex, and they require effort and attention to maintain harmony and intimacy. However, when issues arise, it is essential to address them rather than let them fester and potentially damage the relationship. Through psychodynamic therapy, clients can gain a deeper understanding of themselves and their relationships, leading to healing and growth. As we continue to navigate our relationships, let us remember the words of American author Mignon McLaughlin, "A successful marriage requires falling in love many times, always with the same person." The same can be said for any relationship - it requires continuous effort and a willingness to grow and heal together.

Chapter 14: Family Dynamics and Interpersonal Patterns

In psychodynamic therapy, the family has a significant impact on an individual's psychological development and interpersonal patterns. Understanding the dynamics within a family can provide insight into a client's presenting issue and aid in the therapeutic process.

Family Dynamics and Interpersonal Patterns

Family dynamics refer to the relationships and interactions between family members. These dynamics play a crucial role in shaping an individual's beliefs, values, and behaviors. In psychodynamic therapy, the focus is on exploring the family's history, patterns, and roles to understand how these dynamics have contributed to the client's current interpersonal patterns.

Through family systems theory, we understand that each member of a family has a role and a specific function within the family structure. These roles and functions can either be healthy or dysfunctional, and they can shape how a person relates to others outside of their family. For example, if a child grows up feeling unseen and unheard in their family, they may develop a pattern of seeking out relationships where they struggle to have their needs met. Understanding these patterns is essential in facilitating change and promoting healthy relationships.

Similarly, psychodynamic therapy also emphasizes the importance of early life experiences and attachments in shaping an individual's interpersonal patterns. For instance, a child who has a secure attachment with a caregiver may develop a healthy sense of self and secure attachments with others. In contrast, a child who experiences insecure attachments may struggle with forming relationships and maintaining emotional connections later in life.

As therapists, it is essential to explore these family dynamics and interpersonal patterns as they can provide valuable insight into the client's current struggles. By understanding these dynamics, we can help clients break free from maladaptive patterns and develop healthier ways of relating to others.

Working with Communication and Boundaries

An essential aspect of psychodynamic therapy is improving communication and establishing healthy boundaries within familial relationships. In many cases, communication issues and boundary violations can contribute to conflict and dysfunction within a family.

Therapists can work with clients to identify and address any ineffective communication patterns, such as avoiding difficult conversations or using passive-aggression. By encouraging open and honest communication within the family, we can help improve understanding, promote healthy problem-solving, and build trust.

Boundaries are also crucial in maintaining healthy family dynamics. Without clear boundaries, family members may struggle to maintain their individual needs, leading to resentment and conflict. In psychodynamic therapy, therapists can assist clients in setting boundaries and communicating their needs effectively. Establishing boundaries can help family members develop healthier relationships and promote a sense of independence and autonomy.

Case Examples

To better understand the role of family dynamics and interpersonal patterns in psychodynamic therapy, let's consider a case example. Sarah, a 28-year-old woman, sought therapy for her struggles with codependency in her romantic relationships. Through exploring her family dynamics, it became apparent that Sarah had a history of feeling responsible for her parents' emotions, leading to her difficulty in setting boundaries and taking care of her own needs.

Through therapy, Sarah was able to recognize her patterns and establish healthier boundaries with her parents and in her romantic relationships. They also explored the underlying issues that contributed to her codependency, such as her need for approval and fear of abandonment.

In another case, Thomas, a 42-year-old man, sought therapy for his anger and difficulty maintaining relationships. Through exploring his family dynamics, it became apparent that Thomas had a strained relationship with his father. As a child, Thomas was often criticized and belittled by his father, leading to feelings of inadequacy and unworthiness.

Through therapy, Thomas was able to confront these underlying issues and gain insight into how they have impacted his relationships. With the therapist's guidance, he was able to heal from these past wounds and develop healthier patterns of relating to others.

By understanding the family dynamics and interpersonal patterns at play, therapists can assist clients in breaking free from maladaptive patterns and developing healthier relationships and ways of relating.

In conclusion, family dynamics and interpersonal patterns play a significant role in shaping an individual's psychological development and relationships. By exploring these dynamics in psychodynamic therapy, we can help clients gain insight into their behavior and promote healthier and more fulfilling relationships. By encouraging effective communication and establishing healthy boundaries, we can assist clients in overcoming the impact of dysfunctional family dynamics and develop healthier patterns of relating to others.

Chapter 15: Psychodynamic Therapy for Children and Adolescents

Adaptations of Psychodynamic Therapy for Younger Clients

As we have discussed in previous chapters, psychodynamic therapy focuses on exploring the unconscious mind and uncovering past experiences and traumas that may be influencing current behaviors and emotions. While this approach is effective for adults, it may need to be adapted when working with younger clients, as they may not have the same level of insight and verbal capabilities.

One way to adapt psychodynamic therapy for children and adolescents is by using play therapy. Play is a natural form of expression for children, and through play, therapists can gain insight into their thoughts and feelings. For example, a child may use dolls to act out a traumatic experience, providing the therapist with valuable information that can be explored further in subsequent sessions. Another adaptation for younger clients is the use of imagery or storytelling. By using their imagination, children can express themselves in ways that they may struggle to do verbally. This can help them communicate their thoughts and feelings and gain a better understanding of their experiences.

Techniques and Considerations

In addition to adaptations, there are also specific techniques and considerations that therapists must keep in mind when working with children and adolescents in psychodynamic therapy. These include:

- Establishing a strong therapeutic relationship: It is crucial for therapists to establish a trusting and empathetic relationship with their clients, regardless of age. However, this is especially important for younger clients who may have had previous negative experiences with therapy or struggle to open up with adults.

- Using developmentally appropriate language: Therapists must use age-appropriate language when discussing concepts and experiences with younger clients. This not only helps them understand better but also allows them to express themselves more effectively.

- Flexibility in session structure: While consistency is essential in therapy, it is also essential to be flexible when working with younger clients. This may mean altering the structure of sessions to accommodate their attention spans or incorporating activities that keep them engaged.

- Involving parents or guardians: When working with children and adolescents, therapists must involve parents or guardians in the process. They not only provide valuable insight into their child's life but also facilitate the generalization of therapeutic gains outside of sessions.

Case Examples

To provide a better understanding of how psychodynamic therapy can be adapted for younger clients, let us explore two case examples.

Case 1: Sarah, age 9, was referred to therapy due to her recent change in behavior at school. She had become withdrawn and anxious, and her grades had started to decline. In the initial session, Sarah struggled to articulate her feelings, but through play, she expressed feelings of anger and sadness towards her parents' recent divorce. Through subsequent sessions, Sarah was able to work through her feelings, and her behavior and grades improved.

Case 2: Mark, age 14, was struggling with low self-esteem and an eating disorder. In therapy, he was initially resistant and dismissive, stating that he did not know why he was being forced to attend. However, through storytelling and drawing, Mark revealed underlying feelings of inadequacy and pressure to meet societal expectations. With the help of therapy, Mark was able to build his self-esteem and develop healthier coping mechanisms for his eating disorder.

In both of these cases, adapting psychodynamic therapy to the individual needs of the clients proved beneficial in addressing their underlying issues.

In conclusion, while the core principles of psychodynamic therapy remain the same, it must be adapted to meet the unique needs of children and adolescents. By incorporating play, imagery, and developmentally appropriate techniques, therapists can help younger clients gain insight into their unconscious thoughts and behaviors, leading to positive growth and change.

Chapter 16: Psychodynamic Therapy for Addiction

Understanding Addiction from a Psychodynamic Perspective

Addiction is a complex and multifaceted issue that has significant impacts on individuals and their loved ones. From a traditional psychodynamic perspective, addiction is viewed as a result of unconscious conflicts, emotional distress, and unresolved childhood experiences. These unconscious conflicts and emotional distress can lead individuals to turn to substances or behaviors as a means of coping and self-soothing. In psychodynamic therapy, understanding the individual's underlying issues and addressing them is crucial in treating addiction.

One of the key concepts in psychodynamic therapy is the idea of the unconscious mind. This refers to thoughts, feelings, and memories that are outside of an individual's conscious awareness. In the case of addiction, there may be underlying emotional distress or unresolved past traumas that are causing an individual to turn to substances or behaviors as a coping mechanism. Through exploring the unconscious, the therapist can help the client make connections between their current behaviors and their past experiences, providing insight into the underlying issues contributing to their addiction.

Addressing these issues in therapy allows the individual to process and work through them in a safe and supportive environment. This can lead to a better understanding of their triggers and a decrease in the need to turn to addictive behaviors for coping. In addition, exploring the underlying issues can also help individuals improve their self-esteem and develop healthier ways of regulating their emotions.

Addressing Underlying Issues

Addressing underlying issues is a crucial aspect of psychodynamic therapy for addiction. This involves delving into the individual's past experiences, relationships, and any unresolved emotional conflicts that may be contributing to their addictive behaviors. Through the therapeutic relationship, the therapist can provide a safe and non-judgmental space for the client to explore their feelings and experiences.

One aspect of addressing underlying issues is examining the individual's attachment style. This refers to how they relate to others based on their early childhood experiences. Insecure attachment styles, such as anxious or avoidant, have been linked to a higher risk of developing addiction. By addressing and improving an individual's attachment style through therapy, they can develop healthier relationships and coping mechanisms, reducing the need for addictive behaviors.

Another important aspect of addressing underlying issues in psychodynamic therapy is exploring the individual's defenses. These are unconscious strategies used to protect oneself from anxiety or distress. However, these defenses can also become detrimental and contribute to addictive behaviors. By becoming aware of these defenses and understanding their origins, individuals can begin to develop healthier coping strategies.

Case Examples

To further illustrate the effectiveness of psychodynamic therapy in treating addiction, let's look at a few case examples.

Samantha had been struggling with alcohol addiction for several years. In therapy, she explored her past experiences and discovered that her parents' divorce when she was a child had left her feeling abandoned. This led her to seek comfort in alcohol, but also made it difficult for her to form and maintain healthy relationships. Through therapy, she was able to work through her abandonment issues and develop healthier ways of coping with her emotions, leading to a decrease in her alcohol consumption.

John had been struggling with a gambling addiction for most of his adult life. Through psychodynamic therapy, he was able to make connections between his relationship with his father and his need for constant excitement and risk-taking. He discovered that he had been using gambling as a way to fill an emotional void caused by a distant and emotionally unavailable father. Through therapy, he was able to confront and work through his father issues, leading to a decrease in his gambling behaviors.

These are just a few examples of how psychodynamic therapy can effectively treat addiction by addressing underlying issues. By providing a supportive and introspective space, individuals can gain a better understanding of their addictive behaviors and develop healthier coping strategies.

In conclusion, addiction is a complex issue that requires a holistic approach to treatment. From a psychodynamic perspective, it is vital to understand the individual's underlying issues and address them in therapy. By exploring the unconscious and working through past traumas and conflicts, individuals can develop healthier coping strategies and reduce the need for addictive behaviors. With the help of a skilled and compassionate therapist, individuals can overcome their addiction and lead fulfilling lives.

Chapter 17: Psychodynamic Therapy for Eating Disorders

The Role of Early Experiences in the Development of Eating Disorders

Eating disorders are complex and pervasive mental health issues that can have severe consequences on an individual's physical, emotional, and relational well-being. While many factors contribute to the development of an eating disorder, psychodynamic theory suggests that early experiences have a significant influence.

In the psychodynamic perspective, early experiences, particularly in childhood, shape an individual's sense of self and their relationship with others. For individuals with eating disorders, early experiences involving attachment, rejection, control, and trauma can contribute to distorted perceptions of self and difficulties in regulating emotions.

For example, an individual who experienced neglect or rejection from a caregiver may develop a deep-seated fear of abandonment. This fear may lead them to believe that they are unworthy of love and that they need to control their body and food intake to be accepted and loved. On the other hand, individuals who experienced traumatic events such as physical or sexual abuse may use disordered eating as a coping mechanism to numb painful emotions and regain a sense of control.

Furthermore, early experiences with body image and weight can also play a significant role in the development of an eating disorder. Negative comments from caregivers or peers, exposure to unrealistic body standards in media, or childhood weight stigma can all contribute to the development of body dissatisfaction and obsessive thoughts about food and weight.

Addressing Body Image and Self-esteem

In psychodynamic therapy for eating disorders, one of the primary goals is to help individuals develop a healthier relationship with their bodies and improve self-esteem.

This involves exploring early experiences and understanding the underlying emotional needs and dynamics that contribute to negative body image and self-esteem.

Therapists may use techniques such as mirroring and idealization to help clients build a more positive and accurate image of themselves. They may also help individuals identify and challenge negative thoughts and beliefs about their bodies, as well as explore alternative ways of meeting their emotional needs.

Interventions in psychodynamic therapy also focus on improving self-esteem, which may have been damaged by past experiences. Through therapy, individuals can develop a more realistic and compassionate view of themselves, allowing them to value their worth beyond their appearance or weight.

Additionally, building a healthy sense of self and self-worth can also help individuals establish better boundaries, assert their needs, and develop healthier relationships with others.

Case Examples

Case 1:
Sarah, a 25-year-old woman, was diagnosed with anorexia nervosa at the age of

19. She had a tumultuous relationship with her mother, who was highly critical of her appearance and weight. Sarah believed that she had to be thin to receive love and affection. In therapy, Sarah explored her early experiences and realized that her mother's comments were rooted in her own struggles with body image and self-esteem. As Sarah worked through her negative emotions and developed a healthier sense of self, she was able to challenge her distorted beliefs and establish healthier boundaries with her mother.

Case 2:
John, a 32-year-old man, had a history of binge eating disorder. In therapy, John recalled how his father would constantly make comments about his weight and restrict his food intake as a child. John also experienced traumatic events in his teenage years, leading him to turn to food for comfort. In therapy, John was able to connect his disordered eating behaviors to his need to regain control in his life and cope with past traumas. Through therapy, John was able to identify healthier coping strategies, build

self-esteem, and establish better self-care practices.

Overall, these case examples demonstrate how early experiences can influence the development of eating disorders and how psychodynamic therapy can help individuals understand and address underlying emotional needs and dynamics that contribute to disordered eating behaviors.

Conclusion

Eating disorders are not solely based on food and weight, but rather deeply rooted in early experiences, attachment, and self-perception. Psychodynamic therapy offers a comprehensive approach to addressing the complexities of eating disorders, exploring the underlying dynamics and emotional needs, and guiding individuals towards a healthier relationship with themselves and their bodies. By understanding the role of early experiences and addressing body image and self-esteem, individuals can reclaim their sense of self and lead fulfilling lives.

Chapter 18: Psychodynamic Therapy for Sexual Issues

Sexuality, like any other aspect of human experience, can be influenced by various factors and can manifest in different ways. In clinical psychology, sexual issues are commonly addressed through psychodynamic therapy, which aims to understand the underlying psychological dynamics that contribute to sexual dysfunction, paraphilias, and gender identity concerns. Through this therapeutic approach, individuals can gain a deeper understanding of their sexual experiences and develop healthier ways of expressing their sexuality.

Understanding and Addressing Sexual Dysfunction

Sexual dysfunction refers to difficulties with sexual desire, arousal, or orgasm that cause significant distress or problems in a person's relationships. This can include disorders such as erectile dysfunction, premature ejaculation, and hypoactive sexual desire disorder. While these issues can have physical causes, they may also be linked to underlying psychological factors.

In psychodynamic therapy, the focus is on exploring the individual's unconscious thoughts, feelings, and experiences that may be contributing to their sexual difficulties. For example, a person with erectile dysfunction may have unresolved feelings of anger or resentment towards their partner, leading to difficulties with arousal. By addressing these underlying issues, individuals can better understand and work through their sexual difficulties.

In addition to addressing individual psychological factors, psychodynamic therapy also looks at the influence of societal and cultural norms on sexuality. For example, certain beliefs and expectations about gender roles and performance can contribute to sexual dysfunction. By exploring these cultural influences, individuals can challenge and reframe harmful attitudes and beliefs, promoting healthier sexual expression.

Paraphilias and Gender Identity

Paraphilias refer to sexual behaviors and interests that are outside of societal norms and may cause distress or harm to oneself or others. This can include exhibitionism, voyeurism, and pedophilia. Similarly, gender identity refers to a person's internal sense of being male, female, or non-binary, and how it aligns with their assigned sex at birth.

In psychodynamic therapy, individuals with paraphilias and gender identity concerns are supported in exploring their unconscious motivations and experiences that shape their sexual desires and identity. This can involve understanding past traumas or conflicts that may have influenced their sexual interests or the development of their gender identity.

Furthermore, psychodynamic therapy can help identify and address any underlying shame or guilt surrounding these issues. By creating a non-judgmental and supportive therapeutic environment, individuals can freely explore their sexual and gender identity, leading to increased self-acceptance and a healthier sense of self.

Case Examples

One case example of utilizing psychodynamic therapy for sexual issues is with a 35-year-old man struggling with premature ejaculation. In therapy, it became apparent that he had internalized messages from his conservative upbringing that sex was shameful and should only be done for procreation. This created feelings of anxiety and guilt during sexual encounters, leading to premature ejaculation. Through therapy, he was able to challenge these beliefs and develop a healthier understanding of sexuality, leading to improved sexual functioning and intimacy with his partner.

Another example is a 22-year-old woman who identified as a lesbian, but struggled with feelings of shame and confusion about her sexual orientation. Through psychodynamic therapy, it was discovered that she had unresolved issues with her father, who had frequently made homophobic remarks during her childhood. By exploring and processing these feelings surrounding her relationship with her father, she was able to confidently embrace her sexual orientation and experience a more fulfilling and authentic sense of self.

In both of these examples, psychodynamic therapy helped individuals understand and address their underlying psychological dynamics that were contributing to their sexual difficulties and promote a healthier and more satisfying sexual expression.

Overall, psychodynamic therapy provides a unique and insightful approach to addressing sexual issues by exploring the unconscious motivations and experiences that contribute to an individual's sexual expression. By creating a safe and nonjudgmental space, individuals can gain a deeper understanding of their sexuality and develop healthier ways of expressing it.

Chapter 19: Integrating Cultural Competence in Psychodynamic Therapy

While psychodynamic therapy may have originated in Western cultures, it is important for therapists to recognize and integrate cultural competence in their practice. This involves understanding and respecting the beliefs, values, and behaviors of diverse cultural groups and how they may impact the therapeutic process. In this chapter, we will explore the role of culture in psychodynamic therapy and how therapists can effectively integrate cultural competence into their practice.

Understanding Cultural Competence

Cultural competence is a dynamic process that involves being aware of one's own cultural values and biases, as well as those of the client. It is not about memorizing different cultural practices, but rather having an open and non-judgmental attitude towards diverse cultural backgrounds. This includes acknowledging the power dynamics and systemic inequalities that may exist between the therapist and the client.

As therapists, it is our responsibility to recognize our own cultural norms and how they may impact our perception of the client and their experiences. A lack of cultural competence can lead to misunderstandings, misinterpretations, or even harm to the therapeutic relationship. It is therefore crucial for therapists to continuously educate themselves and be open to learning about different cultures.

Addressing Power and Privilege in the Therapeutic Relationship

The therapeutic relationship is central to psychodynamic therapy and it is important to acknowledge the power dynamics at play. As therapists, we hold a position of power and privilege over our clients, which may be heightened in the context of a culturally diverse therapeutic relationship. It is important to recognize and address these power dynamics to create a safe and equitable therapeutic environment.

One way to address power and privilege is by actively acknowledging and exploring our own biases and assumptions that may impact how we view and interact with our clients. This can involve engaging in self-reflection and seeking supervision or consultation from colleagues. Engaging in open and honest communication with clients about these power dynamics can also be beneficial in building a trusting therapeutic relationship.

The Importance of Cultural Humility

Cultural humility involves recognizing that we all hold biases and are constantly learning and evolving in our understanding of different cultures. It is important to approach each client with an open mind and a willingness to learn from them. This can involve asking questions, actively listening, and being open to feedback and correction from clients.

Cultural humility also involves being aware of the impact of systemic inequalities and actively working towards addressing them. This may involve advocating for clients and being aware of the barriers they may face in accessing mental health services.

Integrating Cultural Competence in Practice

Integrating cultural competence in psychodynamic therapy involves understanding the complexities and nuances of different cultural backgrounds and how they may impact therapeutic processes. This can include considering culture in the assessment process, adapting techniques to fit the client's cultural background, and being aware of potential cultural transference and countertransference.

It is also important to create a safe and inclusive therapeutic environment for clients, which may involve being flexible in terms of communication and being open to incorporating cultural practices in therapy. This can help clients feel understood and validated in their individual experiences.

Challenges and Critiques

As with any approach to therapy, integrating cultural competence in psychodynamic therapy is not without its challenges and critiques. Some critics argue that focusing on culture may ignore underlying psychodynamic issues, while others argue that cultural competence should not be treated as a checklist but rather a continuous process of learning and self-reflection.

It is important for therapists to acknowledge and address these critiques while also recognizing the importance of cultural competence in providing effective and ethical therapy.

The Impact on the Therapist and the Client

Integrating cultural competence in psychodynamic therapy not only benefits the client, but also the therapist. By being aware of our own cultural biases and limitations, therapists can expand their understanding and approach to therapy. This can lead to a deeper understanding of the client and their experiences, as well as a more enriching therapeutic relationship.

For clients, cultural competence in therapy can lead to a greater sense of validation and understanding of their cultural identity. This can also help reduce the stigma and barriers to accessing therapy within diverse communities.

Conclusion

In conclusion, cultural competence is a crucial aspect of providing effective and ethical psychodynamic therapy. By acknowledging and addressing power dynamics and actively integrating cultural humility in practice, therapists can create a safe and inclusive environment for clients from diverse cultural backgrounds. By continuously engaging in self-reflection and ongoing education, therapists can enhance their understanding and approach to therapy.

Chapter 20: Ethical and Professional Issues in Psychodynamic Therapy

Dual Relationships

As therapists, our primary responsibility is to our clients and their well-being. This means maintaining boundaries and avoiding any potential conflicts of interest, including dual relationships. Dual relationships refer to situations where a therapist has a professional relationship with a client while also having another type of relationship, such as a personal or business relationship. In psychodynamic therapy, where the therapeutic relationship is at the core of the treatment, it is especially crucial to be aware of and avoid dual relationships.

It can be tempting for therapists to engage in dual relationships, particularly with clients who evoke strong emotional responses. However, it is important to remember that engaging in any type of dual relationship can create a power imbalance and jeopardize the therapeutic relationship. For example, a therapist may feel obligated to provide special treatment or favors to a client they have a personal relationship with, leading to ethical and professional boundary violations. Therefore, it is essential for therapists to maintain clear boundaries and prioritize their clients' well-being over their own personal needs.

Self-disclosure

Self-disclosure is the act of therapists revealing personal information about themselves to their clients during therapy sessions. In psychodynamic therapy, where the focus is on uncovering unconscious thoughts and feelings, self-disclosure can be a powerful tool. It can help build trust and rapport with the client, create a sense of mutual understanding and empathy, and model vulnerability for the client. However, self-disclosure can also create ethical and professional dilemmas if not done carefully and thoughtfully.

Therapists must consider the purpose and potential impact of their self-disclosure before sharing personal information with their clients. They must also be mindful of whether their self-disclosure is for the benefit of the client or for their own needs. For example, sharing a personal experience that is relevant and helpful to the client's therapeutic journey can be beneficial, but sharing personal information that is solely for the therapist's self-gratification can be unethical.

Confidentiality and Boundaries

Confidentiality and boundaries are fundamental ethical principles in therapy, and they are particularly important in psychodynamic therapy, where clients may discuss sensitive and deeply personal information. Confidentiality refers to the strict privacy and protection of the client's information, and boundaries refer to the limits of the therapeutic relationship. As therapists, it is our ethical and professional responsibility to uphold these principles and create a safe and trusting space for our clients to share and process their thoughts and feelings.

In psychodynamic therapy, where the boundaries can be less rigid due to the nature of the therapy, it is crucial to continuously assess and maintain boundaries. This includes avoiding any physical contact with clients, maintaining appropriate dress and appearance, and setting and adhering to strict communication guidelines. Additionally, therapists must also be aware of confidentiality breaches, especially in cases where they may need to disclose client information, such as in cases of harm to self or others.

Ethical Decision-making

There is no one-size-fits-all approach to ethical decision-making in psychodynamic therapy, as each therapist may have their own values, beliefs, and personal boundaries. However, there are ethical principles and guidelines that all therapists must follow to ensure their clients' well-being and professional integrity. These include adhering to professional codes of ethics, regularly attending supervision, and seeking consultation when faced with ethical dilemmas.

In psychodynamic therapy, where there may be fewer rules and more gray areas, it is essential to regularly reflect on one's values and beliefs and how they may influence the therapeutic process. Therapists must also continuously assess the power dynamics in the therapeutic relationship and be aware of how their actions and decisions may impact their clients. Being mindful, self-reflective, and seeking feedback from supervisors and colleagues can aid in ethical decision-making and ensure the best outcomes for clients.

As therapists, we must never underestimate the power of the therapeutic relationship and the ethical and professional responsibilities that come with it. By adhering to ethical principles and continuously reflecting on our actions, decisions, and boundaries, we can provide the best possible care for our clients while maintaining our professional integrity.

Chapter 21: Integration of Neuroscientific Findings in Psychodynamic Theory

Introduction

Over the years, the field of clinical psychology has been greatly influenced by various scientific disciplines, including neurobiology. With advancements in technology and research, there has been an increasing interest in understanding the neurobiological underpinnings of psychological disorders and their treatment. In this chapter, we will explore the integration of neuroscientific findings in psychodynamic theory, the implications for clinical practice, and future directions for this integration.

Neuroscientific Contributions to Psychodynamic Theory

Traditionally, psychodynamic theory focused on unconscious processes and the influence of early childhood experiences on the development of psychopathology. However, recent neuroscientific research has shed light on the neural mechanisms underlying these processes. For example, studies have shown that traumatic experiences can lead to changes in the brain's structure and functioning, particularly in the regions involved in emotion regulation and stress response. Furthermore, neuroimaging studies have provided evidence for the existence of unconscious processes, supporting key concepts of psychodynamic theory, such as repression and defense mechanisms. By using advanced imaging techniques, researchers have been able to map out the neural pathways associated with these unconscious processes, deepening our understanding of how they manifest in psychological disorders.

Neuroscientific findings have also led to a better understanding of the therapeutic relationship and its role in the healing process. For example, studies have shown that the bond between therapist and client can have a significant impact on the brain's reward and attachment systems, further emphasizing the importance of the therapeutic alliance in psychodynamic therapy.

Implications for Practice

The integration of neuroscientific findings in psychodynamic theory has significant implications for clinical practice. First and foremost, it highlights the need for therapists to have a basic understanding of neurobiology and its relevance to mental health. By incorporating this knowledge into their practice, therapists can enhance their treatment approach and better understand the underlying neurobiological processes at play in their clients. Moreover, this integration has the potential to bridge the gap between psychodynamic theory and other evidence-based approaches, such as cognitive-behavioral therapy. By incorporating neuroscientific principles, therapists can better tailor their treatment plans to fit the individual needs of their clients, increasing the effectiveness of psychodynamic therapy.

Another implication is the potential for a more interdisciplinary approach to treatment. By collaborating with neuroscientists, therapists can gain a deeper understanding of the neurobiological mechanisms involved in psychological disorders and their treatment. This collaboration can lead to the development of more effective treatment interventions and a greater understanding of the complex relationship between the brain and behavior.

Future Directions

As the field of neuroscience continues to advance, the integration of these findings into psychodynamic theory is expected to further evolve. One direction for future research is the exploration of the impact of attachment styles on the neural pathways involved in the therapeutic relationship. Studies have shown that individuals with secure attachment styles are more likely to experience positive changes in their brain's reward and attachment systems during therapy, highlighting the importance of examining attachment processes in the context of therapy.

Another area of interest is the use of neurofeedback techniques in psychodynamic therapy. Neurofeedback, a form of biofeedback, allows individuals to modify their brain activity through real-time feedback. By incorporating these techniques into psychodynamic therapy, clients may have a more active role in the therapeutic process, leading to improved treatment outcomes.

Furthermore, the integration of neuroscientific findings has significant potential in the field of prevention and early intervention. By identifying neural markers of vulnerability to certain disorders, it may be possible to intervene early on and prevent the development of more severe psychological symptoms.

Conclusion

In conclusion, the integration of neuroscientific findings in psychodynamic theory is a promising direction for the field of clinical psychology. By deepening our understanding of neural mechanisms underlying psychological processes, therapists can enhance their practice and improve treatment outcomes for their clients. As research continues to advance and new findings emerge, the integration of neuroscience and psychodynamic theory is expected to further broaden our understanding of human behavior and the treatment of psychological disorders.

Chapter 22: The Evidence for Psychodynamic Therapy

Psychodynamic therapy has been considered a foundational approach in the field of clinical psychology for over a century. Despite its long history, the effectiveness of this therapeutic approach has been met with skepticism and scrutiny. In this chapter, we will explore the latest research supporting the effectiveness of psychodynamic therapy, as well as critiques and limitations that have been raised. We will also discuss the implications for clinical practice and how this evidence can inform and improve the use of psychodynamic therapy in treating clients.

Research Supporting the Effectiveness of Psychodynamic Therapy

Over the years, various studies have been conducted to determine the efficacy of psychodynamic therapy. One of the most comprehensive and renowned studies is the Clarkin et al. study published in the American Journal of Psychiatry in

2007. This study followed 488 patients who received psychodynamic therapy for a range of psychological disorders, including depression, anxiety, personality disorders, and substance abuse. The results showed that 69% of patients showed significant improvement after 12 months of therapy, and this improvement continued over a five-year follow-up period. This study is among many others that demonstrate the effectiveness of psychodynamic therapy in treating various mental health issues.

Moreover, research has shown that psychodynamic therapy is not only effective in treating a wide range of disorders but also has lasting effects. In a meta-analysis conducted by Leichsenring and Rabung (2008), it was found that the effects of psychodynamic therapy remained stable and maintained or even improved after the end of treatment. This is particularly significant as it indicates that psychodynamic therapy not only provides short-term relief but also produces long-term benefits for patients.

Critiques and Limitations

Despite the growing body of evidence supporting the effectiveness of psychodynamic therapy, critics have raised several objections to this approach. Some have argued that psychodynamic therapy relies too heavily on subjective interpretations of unconscious drives and childhood experiences, lacking empirical evidence to support its principles. Another critique is the length and intensity of the therapy, with some sessions lasting for years and focusing on unconscious processes, which can be frustrating for clients seeking immediate relief.

Additionally, criticisms have been directed towards the approach's emphasis on the therapist as an expert and the power dynamics between the therapist and the client. It has been argued that this may lead to unequal power dynamics and can potentially harm clients. Furthermore, some critics have raised concerns about the lack of inclusivity in psychodynamic therapy, with its theories and techniques being based on a Western, individualistic perspective.

Implications for Clinical Practice

Despite the limitations and critiques, the evidence for the effectiveness of psychodynamic therapy cannot be ignored. As psychologists, it is essential to critically evaluate and incorporate evidence-based practices into our clinical work. The research supporting the effectiveness of psychodynamic therapy can inform and enhance our understanding and usage of this approach.

One significant implication of the evidence is the importance of establishing a strong therapeutic relationship in psychodynamic therapy. Studies have shown that the therapeutic alliance is one of the most important factors contributing to the effectiveness of this approach. As such, therapists must focus on building a trusting and collaborative relationship with their clients to facilitate positive outcomes.

Additionally, the evidence suggests that psychodynamic therapy can be effective for various mental health issues, highlighting its versatility. This means that psychodynamic therapy can be utilized in conjunction with other therapeutic approaches to address the complexity of clients' needs. It also emphasizes the need for therapists to be flexible and adaptable in their approach, tailoring treatment to suit the individual needs and goals of each client.

Another implication for clinical practice is the need for therapists to continuously reflect on their use of power and privilege in the therapeutic relationship. This involves being aware of potential power imbalances and actively working to create a safe and equitable space for clients to explore their thoughts, feelings, and experiences.

In conclusion, the evidence for the effectiveness of psychodynamic therapy is substantial, despite its limitations and critiques. As psychologists, it is crucial to weigh this evidence and incorporate it into our clinical practice to provide the best possible care to our clients. The research also highlights the importance of ongoing self-reflection, cultural competence, and collaboration in delivering psychodynamic therapy effectively. By utilizing the evidence and continuously adapting our approach, we can continue to evolve and improve the use of psychodynamic therapy in our work with clients.

Chapter 23: Integrating Psychodynamic Therapy with Other Approaches

Complementary Approaches

Integrating psychodynamic therapy with other approaches can be a powerful tool in helping clients address their mental health concerns. In recent years, there has been a growing emphasis on evidence-based practices and the use of different therapeutic modalities in the field of psychology. While some may view this as a threat to the traditional psychodynamic approach, many therapists have embraced the integration of different techniques and approaches to better serve their clients.

One complementary approach to psychodynamic therapy is cognitive-behavioral therapy (CBT). CBT focuses on the relationship between thoughts, emotions, and behaviors, and how they can impact each other. This approach is often used to help individuals identify and challenge negative thoughts and behaviors that may be contributing to their mental health concerns. By combining CBT with psychodynamic therapy, therapists can help clients gain insight into their underlying thoughts and beliefs while also learning practical coping skills.

Another approach that can complement psychodynamic therapy is mindfulness-based therapies. Mindfulness practices teach individuals to be more present and aware of their thoughts and emotions, without judgment. This can be particularly helpful in psychodynamic therapy, as it allows clients to observe their internal experiences and gain a deeper understanding of their underlying emotions and motivations.

Challenges and Benefits of Integration

Integrating different therapeutic modalities can present some challenges for therapists. Each approach has its own theories and techniques, and merging them together can be complex. It takes skill and knowledge to determine when and how to integrate different techniques in a way that is most beneficial for the client.

However, the benefits of integrating psychodynamic therapy with other approaches are numerous. Combining techniques from different modalities can enhance the therapeutic process and address a wider range of mental health concerns. For example, a client struggling with depression may benefit from both the insight gained in psychodynamic therapy and the practical coping skills taught in CBT. Additionally, using different approaches can increase client engagement and motivation, as they may connect more with one approach over another.

Integrating psychodynamic therapy with other approaches may also increase the effectiveness of treatment. As therapists gain a comprehensive understanding of their client's internal experiences, they are better equipped to tailor the therapeutic approach to meet their specific needs. By using multiple approaches, therapists are better able to address the complexities and nuances of each individual.

Case Examples

To illustrate the benefits of integration, here are a few brief case examples:

Katie, a 35-year-old woman, comes to therapy seeking help for anxiety and relationship issues. In her psychodynamic therapy sessions, she explores her childhood and the impact it has had on her relationships in adulthood. However, she struggles to manage her anxious thoughts, and her therapist decides to integrate CBT techniques to help her challenge and reframe these thoughts. As a result, Katie experiences decreased anxiety and increased confidence in her relationships.

John, a 45-year-old man, has been in therapy for a few months, working on his depression and low self-esteem. While the psychodynamic approach has helped him gain insight into why he feels the way he does, his therapist notices that he is often self-critical and struggles with negative self-talk. His therapist integrates mindfulness-based practices into their sessions, helping John become more aware of his thoughts and emotions without judgment. This leads to a decrease in his negative self-talk and an increase in self-compassion.

Sarah, a 21-year-old college student, is struggling with binge-eating and negative body image. While her psychodynamic therapist helps her explore the underlying emotional reasons for her behaviors, she also struggles with managing her binge episodes. With her therapist's guidance, she begins incorporating techniques from dialectical behavior therapy (DBT) into her daily life, such as mindfulness, emotion regulation, and distress tolerance. As a result, she is able to better cope with her emotions, leading to a decrease in her binge-eating episodes.

These are just a few examples of how the integration of different therapeutic modalities can benefit clients. As therapists continue to explore and integrate different approaches, the possibilities for helping their clients grow and heal are endless.

In Conclusion

In conclusion, integrating psychodynamic therapy with other approaches can enhance the therapeutic process and lead to better outcomes for clients. While this approach may present some challenges, the benefits far outweigh them. As therapists continue to explore and integrate different techniques and approaches, the field of psychology will continue to evolve, leading to more effective and comprehensive treatment options for clients.

Chapter 24: The Importance of Supervision in Psychodynamic Therapy

Supervision plays a crucial role in the development and practice of psychodynamic therapy. It is a vital component that ensures the effectiveness and ethical practice of therapists. In this chapter, we will explore the significance of supervision in psychodynamic therapy, essential skills and competencies for supervisors, and provide case examples to illustrate the benefits of supervision.

Importance of Supervision

Supervision in psychodynamic therapy is a collaborative and reflective process between therapists and their supervisors. It serves as a platform for therapists to receive guidance, support, and feedback on their practice. With the therapist being the instrument of change in therapy, supervision ensures that they are able to maintain their own well-being and utilize their skills effectively. One of the key benefits of supervision is enhancing the therapist's self-awareness. Through supervision, therapists can reflect on their own countertransference, biases, and assumptions that may interfere with the therapeutic process. Self-awareness allows therapists to identify their blind spots and address any personal issues that may affect their work with clients.

Supervision also facilitates the growth and development of therapists. It provides a safe space for therapists to discuss difficult cases, explore new techniques, and receive constructive feedback from their supervisors. This enables therapists to continuously improve their skills and provide the best possible care to their clients.

Moreover, supervision helps to maintain ethical and professional standards in therapy. Therapists can seek guidance from their supervisors on ethical dilemmas, boundary issues, and confidentiality concerns. This ensures that therapists are practicing within their scope of competency and upholding the well-being of their clients.

Essential Skills and Competencies

Supervisors play a crucial role in guiding and supporting therapists in their professional development. It requires a specific set of skills and competencies to effectively supervise therapists in psychodynamic therapy. Some of the key skills and competencies include:

- Knowledge and understanding of psychodynamic theory and practice: Supervisors must have a strong foundation in psychodynamic theory and practice to effectively guide therapists in their work with clients.

- Clinical expertise: Supervisors should have ample experience in psychodynamic therapy and possess advanced clinical skills to provide guidance and feedback to therapists.

- Case conceptualization: The ability to conceptualize cases from a psychodynamic perspective is crucial for guiding therapists in their work with clients. Supervisors should be able to help therapists understand the underlying dynamics and themes in their clients' behaviors.

- Reflection and self-awareness: Just as therapists need to be self-aware, supervisors must also possess a high level of self-awareness to effectively guide therapists in their work. They should be able to recognize their own biases, countertransference, and emotional reactions in the supervisory process.

- Communication and feedback: Effective communication skills are essential for supervisors to provide constructive feedback to therapists. They should be able to provide feedback in a non-judgmental and supportive manner.

- Cultural competency: With the increasing diversity of clients seeking therapy, supervisors must possess cultural competence to guide therapists in working with clients from different backgrounds.

Case Examples

To illustrate the benefits of supervision in psychodynamic therapy, let us look at two case examples:

Case 1:

Samantha, a young therapist, has been seeing a client, Mary, who presents with depression and anxiety. After several sessions, Samantha notices that she is feeling overwhelmed with intense feelings of sadness and helplessness. In supervision, Samantha discusses her countertransference reactions towards Mary and realizes that her own personal struggles with depression were influencing her work with Mary. With the support and guidance of her supervisor, Samantha was able to address her personal issues and continue working with Mary effectively.

Case 2:

Mark, an experienced therapist, has been struggling with a client, James, who has a history of trauma. In supervision, Mark shares his frustrations with James, finding him resistant to therapy and not making any progress. Through reflective discussions with his supervisor, Mark realizes that he has been approaching James' trauma from a cognitive-behavioral perspective rather than a psychodynamic one. With this insight, Mark changes his approach and sees significant progress in James' therapy.

In both cases, supervision helped the therapists to identify and address their personal issues and find better ways to work with their clients. Without supervision, these therapists may have continued to struggle and potentially harm their clients.

In conclusion, supervision is an essential aspect of psychodynamic therapy that benefits both therapists and clients. It facilitates the growth and development of therapists, maintains ethical and professional standards, and ensures the delivery of effective therapy. By providing a supportive and reflective space, supervision enables therapists to continuously improve their skills and provide competent and ethical care to their clients.

Chapter 25: Burnout Prevention and Self-care in Psychodynamic Therapy

Impact of Therapist's Emotional Investment

As therapists, we are constantly invested in our clients' emotional well-being. We listen, empathize, and hold space for our clients' deepest pain and vulnerabilities. Our work requires us to be emotionally present and attuned, which can be both emotionally and physically exhausting. This emotional investment can take a toll on our own well-being, leading to burnout and compassion fatigue.

In psychodynamic therapy, the therapist's emotional investment is a crucial aspect of the therapeutic relationship. It is our willingness to genuinely connect with our clients and explore their internal worlds with empathy and curiosity that allows for the process of healing to occur. However, it is also important to recognize the impact that this emotional investment can have on us as therapists.

When we become too emotionally invested in our clients, we may find ourselves taking on their pain and struggles, which can lead to feelings of being overwhelmed, drained, and even resentful. This can also affect our ability to maintain boundaries and create a safe therapeutic environment. As therapists, it is important to find a balance between being emotionally invested and maintaining our own well-being.

Strategies for Self-care

Self-care is essential for therapists to maintain their emotional and physical well-being. It involves intentionally engaging in activities and practices that promote our overall health and prevent burnout. While self-care looks different for everyone, here are some strategies that can be helpful for therapists in psychodynamic therapy:

1. Self-compassion:
Often as therapists, we are so focused on caring for others that we forget to show ourselves the same kindness and compassion. Practicing self-compassion involves

being kind and understanding towards ourselves, especially during times of stress and self-doubt. It also means acknowledging and validating our own emotions and needs.

2. Setting Boundaries:
In order to prevent burnout, it is important for therapists to set boundaries with their clients. This includes setting clear expectations about session length, frequency, and contact outside of sessions. It also means being aware of our own limits and saying no when necessary.

3. Engaging in Self-care Activities:
It is important for therapists to find activities that bring them joy and relaxation outside of their work. This can include hobbies, exercise, spending time with loved ones, or any activity that helps us recharge and reconnect with ourselves.

4. Seeking Support:
Therapists can also benefit from seeking support from colleagues, supervisors, or a therapist of their own. Having a space to process the challenges of our work and gain perspective can be incredibly helpful in preventing burnout.

Case Examples

As therapists, we may encounter challenging cases and situations that can impact our emotional well-being. Here are some case examples to illustrate the importance of self-care and preventing burnout in psychodynamic therapy:

Case 1:
A therapist has been working with a client who has a history of childhood trauma. The client frequently experiences intense emotional outbursts during sessions, leaving the therapist feeling drained and overwhelmed. Despite setting boundaries and practicing self-care activities, the therapist finds themselves experiencing compassion fatigue and struggling to remain present in sessions. Seeking support from a supervisor and setting clear boundaries with the client allows the therapist to better manage their emotions and continue providing effective therapy.

Case 2:
A therapist has been working with a client with chronic depression for several months. The client recently experienced a major relapse and the therapist finds themselves

taking on the client's pain and feeling hopeless about their progress. The therapist begins to feel overwhelmed and exhausted, leading to decreased motivation and effectiveness in therapy. With the help of self-compassion and self-care practices, the therapist is able to process their emotions and regain their sense of purpose and resilience in working with the client.

In conclusion, the therapist's emotional investment is a crucial aspect of psychodynamic therapy, but it is also important to recognize and manage its potential impact on our well-being. By engaging in self-care practices and maintaining boundaries, we can prevent burnout and continue providing effective and compassionate therapy to our clients. Remember, taking care of ourselves allows us to be the best therapists we can be.

Chapter 26: Relapse Prevention in Psychodynamic Therapy

Understanding Vulnerabilities and Triggers

Relapse prevention is a crucial aspect of psychodynamic therapy, as it aims to help clients maintain their progress and avoid returning to previous unhealthy behaviors and patterns. In order for this to be successful, it is important for therapists and clients to work together to identify potential vulnerabilities and triggers.

One of the key components of psychodynamic therapy is understanding the underlying factors that contribute to a client's problematic behaviors and thought patterns. By delving into the unconscious mind and exploring past experiences and traumas, therapists and clients can gain valuable insight into potential vulnerabilities. These vulnerabilities can include unresolved conflicts, unmet needs, and past traumas that may resurface and trigger problematic behaviors. As therapists, it is important to work with clients to identify and address these vulnerabilities, as they can be powerful triggers for relapse if left unaddressed.

Additionally, therapists and clients must also examine potential external triggers, such as certain people, places, or situations that may evoke strong emotional responses and lead to relapse. By identifying these triggers, therapists can help clients develop coping strategies to avoid or cope with them in a healthy way.

Furthermore, understanding the cyclical nature of triggers and vulnerabilities is also important. For example, past traumas can often lead to negative self-perceptions and low self-esteem, which in turn can create vulnerabilities to relapse. By addressing the root cause of these vulnerabilities, therapists can help clients break this cycle and prevent future relapses.

Developing an Aftercare Plan

In addition to identifying vulnerabilities and triggers, developing an aftercare plan is another crucial aspect of relapse prevention in psychodynamic therapy. After completing therapy, clients may struggle to maintain their progress on their own and may be at risk for relapse. Therefore, it is important to establish an aftercare plan to provide ongoing support and ensure that the progress made in therapy is maintained.

The aftercare plan should be tailored to each individual client and may include elements such as regular therapy sessions, support groups, and developing a strong support network of friends and family. It is also important to address any ongoing challenges or stressors in the client's life and provide them with coping strategies and resources to manage these challenges in a healthy way.

Additionally, therapists should also encourage clients to continue the self-reflection and self-awareness skills learned in therapy, in order to recognize and address any potential triggers or vulnerabilities that may arise. By involving clients in the development of their own aftercare plan, therapists empower them to take an active role in their own relapse prevention.

Case Examples

To further illustrate the importance of relapse prevention in psychodynamic therapy, here are a few case examples:

- Sarah struggled with an eating disorder for several years before seeking therapy. Through psychodynamic therapy, she was able to explore the roots of her disorder and develop a healthier relationship with food and her body. However, after completing therapy, Sarah found that stressful situations at work were triggering her to engage in disordered eating behaviors once again. With the help of her therapist, Sarah was able to identify these triggers and develop coping strategies to manage her stress in a healthy way.

- John had a history of substance abuse and had been sober for two years with the help of psychodynamic therapy. However, when his father passed away unexpectedly, John found himself tempted to turn to substances to cope with the grief and emotional pain. Through therapy, John was able to process his feelings and come to terms with his loss, preventing a relapse and further strengthening his recovery.

- Anna struggled with depression and low self-esteem throughout her life, which often led to low motivation and difficulty in maintaining relationships. Through psychodynamic therapy, she was able to work through her unresolved childhood trauma and develop a more positive self-image. However, when she experienced a difficult breakup, Anna found herself slipping back into old patterns of negative thinking and self-isolation. With the support of her therapist and the coping skills learned in therapy, Anna was able to process her emotions and prevent a relapse into depression. These case examples highlight the importance of addressing vulnerabilities and triggers in preventing relapse, as well as the value of developing an aftercare plan to provide ongoing support and guidance.

In conclusion, relapse prevention is a crucial aspect of psychodynamic therapy, as it aims to help clients maintain their progress and prevent future setbacks. By understanding and addressing potential vulnerabilities and triggers, as well as developing a tailored aftercare plan, therapists can empower their clients to continue their journey towards lasting mental health and well-being. Effective relapse prevention requires ongoing commitment and collaboration between therapists and clients, but the benefits of maintaining progress and avoiding relapse are well worth the effort.

Chapter 27: The Role of Psychodynamic Therapy in Non-clinical Settings

The use of psychodynamic therapy is not limited to traditional clinical settings, but can also be applied in various non-clinical settings such as organizational consultation, education and training, and community mental health. In this chapter, we will explore the unique contributions and applications of psychodynamic therapy in these non-clinical contexts.

Organizational Consultation

In recent years, there has been an increased interest in the application of psychodynamic therapy in organizational consultation. This involves working with organizations to improve their functioning and dynamics, with a focus on the interpersonal relationships and conflicts within the organization. Psychodynamic theories help to understand the unconscious motivations and dynamics within the organization, which can have a significant impact on its productivity and success.

One fundamental concept in organizational consultation is the parallel process, where the dynamics within the organization mirror those of the individuals in the organization. For example, if there is a power struggle between the CEO and a manager, it may be reflective of a similar power struggle between the individual and their internal conflicts. By addressing and exploring these underlying dynamics, psychodynamic therapists can help organizations become more self-aware and address issues that may be hindering their success.

Additionally, psychodynamic therapy can also provide insight into organizational cultures, hierarchies, and communication patterns. This understanding can help identify areas of improvement and facilitate change within the organization. Organizational consultation allows for a unique application of psychodynamic therapy principles and techniques, expanding its effectiveness beyond individual therapy.

Education and Training

Education and training are essential components of the mental health field, and psychodynamic therapy has a significant role to play in this area. Psychodynamic principles and techniques can be incorporated into educational and training programs to deepen students' understanding and skills in working with individuals. By learning about psychodynamic theory, trainees can develop a deeper understanding of the unconscious processes and dynamics that drive human behavior.

Moreover, psychodynamic principles can also be applied in teaching and learning methods to facilitate personal growth and awareness. By encouraging critical self-reflection, students can gain a better understanding of their own personal motivations and biases, which can ultimately improve their effectiveness in working with clients. The incorporation of psychodynamic therapy in education and training can help create a more comprehensive and well-rounded approach to mental health.

Community Mental Health

In non-clinical settings, psychodynamic therapy can also be applied to community mental health initiatives. Community mental health services aim to provide mental health support and treatment to individuals within their community, with a focus on improving overall quality of life. Psychodynamic principles can be integrated into these services to promote long-term healing and address underlying issues that may contribute to mental health concerns.

One way in which psychodynamic therapy can be applied in community mental health is through group therapy. Group therapy provides a setting for individuals to explore and work through their personal issues within a supportive community. Through the group process, members can develop a deeper understanding of their unconscious motivations and how they relate to others, promoting personal growth and healing.

Additionally, psychodynamic therapy can also be utilized in community-based interventions, such as advocacy, outreach, and prevention programs. By understanding the underlying dynamics and social factors that contribute to mental health, psychodynamic therapists can develop more effective interventions that address the root causes of mental health concerns.

In conclusion, the application of psychodynamic therapy in non-clinical settings offers unique and valuable contributions to various contexts. From improving organizational functioning to promoting personal growth and community mental health, psychodynamic therapy has the potential to make a positive impact beyond the individual therapy room. By incorporating psychodynamic principles and techniques into these settings, we can expand the reach and effectiveness of this approach, making a difference in the lives of individuals and communities.

Chapter 28: The Role of Psychodynamic Theory in Crisis Intervention

In the face of a crisis, individuals can be overwhelmed by distressing emotions and feel unable to cope with the situation at hand. As mental health professionals, it is our responsibility to assist these individuals in navigating and processing their experiences. This is where the role of psychodynamic theory in crisis intervention becomes crucial.

Role of Psychodynamic Theory in Crisis Intervention

Psychodynamic theory offers a unique lens through which we can understand and approach crises. It recognizes the complexity of human experience and the underlying unconscious processes that drive our thoughts, feelings, and behaviors. By understanding these underlying dynamics, we can help individuals better process and make sense of their traumatic experiences.

One significant contribution of psychodynamic theory in crisis intervention is its emphasis on the therapeutic relationship. In a crisis, the individual often feels vulnerable and seeks a sense of safety and connection. The therapist's empathetic presence and ability to establish a trusting relationship can significantly impact the individual's ability to cope and recover from the crisis. Therefore, a strong therapeutic alliance built on the foundations of psychodynamic theory can provide a secure base for exploring and addressing the individual's distress.

Another important aspect of psychodynamic theory in crisis intervention is its emphasis on early childhood experiences. Crisis situations, especially those involving trauma, can trigger past unresolved issues and reawaken childhood wounds. A psychodynamic approach recognizes the impact of early experiences on our current functioning and can help individuals make connections between past and present events. By understanding the root causes of their distress, individuals can gain insight into their patterns of behavior and begin to heal from traumatic experiences.

Working with Acute Trauma

Acute trauma refers to a single traumatic event that leaves a lasting impact on an individual's mental and emotional well-being. In crisis intervention, it is essential to understand the dynamics of acute trauma and its effects on an individual's psyche. Psychodynamic theory offers a comprehensive framework for understanding and addressing acute trauma.

Firstly, psychodynamic theory recognizes how trauma can disrupt an individual's sense of self and cause a dissociative response as a defense mechanism. In acute trauma, individuals may experience a sense of detachment from their sense of identity, including their beliefs, values, and memories. A psychodynamic approach can help individuals explore these feelings of detachment and work towards integrating their traumatic experiences into their overall sense of self.

Furthermore, psychodynamic theory also takes into account the impact of traumatic experiences on an individual's relationships. Traumatic events can disrupt an individual's ability to form and maintain healthy relationships, leading to feelings of isolation and disconnection. By exploring these relational dynamics, a psychodynamic therapist can help individuals rebuild their sense of trust and connection with others.

Case Examples

To illustrate the role of psychodynamic theory in crisis intervention, let us consider two case examples.

Case 1: Julia is a survivor of a natural disaster and is experiencing symptoms of post-traumatic stress disorder (PTSD). Through a psychodynamic lens, her therapist recognizes how the disaster has triggered her unresolved childhood trauma of feeling unsafe and helpless. Through therapy, Julia is able to explore and make sense of her past experiences, leading to a reduction in her symptoms and an increase in her sense of control.

Case 2: John is a first responder who has recently been involved in a traumatic event. He is struggling with feelings of guilt and shame and has developed difficulties in his relationships. Through a psychodynamic approach, his therapist helps him understand how his past experiences have shaped his current patterns of behavior. By acknowledging and exploring these dynamics, John is able to move towards a healthier way of coping with his trauma and rebuilding his relationships.

In conclusion, psychodynamic theory plays a critical role in crisis intervention by offering a deep understanding of the individual's experiences and their underlying dynamics. Through the therapeutic relationship and exploration of early childhood experiences, it can assist individuals in navigating and processing their traumatic experiences. By doing so, it allows individuals to not only cope with the crisis at hand but also heal and grow from it.

Chapter 29: Group Therapy and Psychodynamic Approaches

Group therapy is an essential part of psychodynamic treatment, offering a unique and powerful way for individuals to explore their thoughts, emotions, and behaviors in a safe and supportive environment. In this chapter, we will delve into the dynamics of group therapy and how psychodynamic techniques can be applied to enhance its effectiveness. Through group therapy, clients have the opportunity to deeply explore their inner worlds, receive feedback from others, and practice new ways of relating and communicating. So let's dive into the fascinating world of group therapy and its intersection with psychodynamic approaches.

Group Dynamics

The dynamics of a group are complex and ever-changing, shaped by the interactions and relationships among its members. The group itself becomes an entity, with its own identity and personality, that can influence the development and progress of its members. In psychodynamic group therapy, the dynamic among group members is the primary focus of treatment, as it reflects and parallels the dynamics of an individual's inner world. The group offers a microcosm for exploring patterns of behavior, relationships, and conflicts that arise within the group and how they may be influenced by each individual's history and unconscious motivations. One of the key dynamics in group therapy is the concept of transference, which refers to the unconscious feelings and reactions that group members may project onto one another based on past experiences. For example, a group member may react to another member in a similar way they reacted to their parent or authority figure in the past. In this way, the group provides a unique opportunity to work through unresolved conflicts and emotions that may have developed in the past, and to gain insight into their impact on current relationships.

Another important group dynamic is the concept of counter-transference, which refers to the feelings and reactions that arise within the therapist towards group members. It is essential for the therapist to be aware of their counter-transference, as it can provide valuable clues about the group dynamics and the dynamics at play within each individual. Through careful self-reflection and processing with the group, the therapist can utilize their counter-transference to deepen their understanding of the group's dynamics and provide more meaningful interventions.

Techniques and Considerations

As with individual psychodynamic therapy, the therapeutic techniques used in group therapy aim to uncover and explore the unconscious motivations and conflicts within each group member. Some common techniques used in group therapy include free association, dream interpretation, and psychoeducation on psychodynamic principles. These techniques allow for the exploration of emotions, thoughts, and behaviors that may have been inaccessible or misunderstood by group members.

Another important consideration in group therapy is the balance between support and challenge. The group must strike the right balance between providing a supportive and understanding environment and challenging group members to explore and confront difficult issues. Too much support can lead to stagnation, while too much challenge can cause group members to feel overwhelmed and defensive. A skilled therapist can navigate this delicate balance and create a growth-promoting atmosphere within the group.

Cultural considerations are also crucial to keep in mind when conducting group therapy. Each group member brings their unique cultural background and experiences, which may affect their perceptions, reactions, and behaviors in the group. It is essential for the therapist to create a culturally sensitive and inclusive environment, where each group member feels safe and understood.

Case Examples

To illustrate the effectiveness of group therapy and psychodynamic approaches, let's look at a couple of case examples. In a group therapy session, a woman, who was a survivor of childhood abuse, shared her feelings of anger and betrayal towards her parents. Through the group's support, she was able to express her emotions and gain deeper insight into how her past experiences impacted her current relationships. With the therapist's guidance, she was able to confront her parents in a healthy and productive way, leading to improved communication and healing in the family.

In another group, a man struggling with substance abuse found that his patterns of self-sabotage and relapse mirrored the relationship dynamics he had witnessed between his parents. With the help of the group, he was able to work through these underlying issues and develop healthier coping mechanisms. Additionally, the group's support and accountability helped him maintain sobriety and work towards building more fulfilling relationships.

Conclusion

Group therapy is a powerful tool in psychodynamic treatment, providing opportunities for individuals to explore their inner worlds and develop meaningful connections with others. Through the dynamics of the group and the use of psychodynamic techniques, individuals can gain insight, heal from past traumas, and develop healthier ways of relating. As therapists, it is vital to be attuned to the unique dynamics of each group and utilize techniques that promote growth and healing within the group.

Chapter 30: Psychodynamic Therapy for Older Adults

Special Considerations for Working with Elderly Clients

As we age, our thoughts, beliefs, and behaviors may be shaped by a variety of factors including physical health, cognitive abilities, and social support systems. When working with elderly clients, it is important for the therapist to consider these unique circumstances and how they may impact the therapeutic process.

One special consideration for working with older adults is the potential for changes in cognitive functioning. As individuals age, they may experience memory loss, difficulty with concentration, and other cognitive impairments. These changes can affect their ability to participate in therapy and process emotions and thoughts in the same way as a younger client. The therapist must be flexible and understanding, adapting the therapy to fit the cognitive abilities of the client. Additionally, physical health may play a role in the therapeutic process for older adults. Chronic pain, limitations in mobility, and other health concerns may impact a client's ability to attend therapy regularly or participate in certain activities. It is important for the therapist to be aware of these limitations and adjust the therapeutic plan accordingly.

Furthermore, older adults may also face issues related to loss and grief, as they may have experienced significant losses in their lives such as the death of loved ones or physical abilities. The therapist must approach these issues with sensitivity and help the client explore ways to cope with these losses.

Addressing Challenges in Aging

Aging can bring about a multitude of challenges, both for the individual and their loved ones. As therapists, it is important to address these challenges in a supportive and empathetic manner. One of the biggest challenges older adults face is a sense of loss and feelings of isolation. Retirement, decreased physical abilities, and the loss of loved ones can all contribute to these emotions. Psychodynamic therapy can be a valuable tool in helping older adults work through these feelings and find ways to cope with the changes in their lives.

Another challenge that may arise is the fear of death and dying. Many older adults may have a heightened awareness of their mortality, which can lead to anxiety, depression, and other mental health concerns. The therapist must create a safe space for the client to explore these thoughts and feelings and provide support in addressing them.

In addition, older adults may also experience difficulty in adjusting to new roles and identities as they transition into retirement or lose physical capabilities. The therapist can assist in this process by helping the client explore their sense of self and find new ways to find meaning and purpose in their lives.

Case Examples

To illustrate the unique considerations and challenges of working with elderly clients in psychodynamic therapy, below are two case examples.

Case One:
Mr. S is a 72-year-old man who recently retired from a successful career in finance. He has been experiencing increased feelings of depression and anxiety since his retirement, as he feels lost and without purpose. In therapy, Mr. S explores his fear of aging and his struggle with adjusting to a new identity outside of his career. Through psychodynamic therapy, he is able to gain a deeper understanding of his feelings and find new ways to find meaning and purpose in his life.

Case Two:
Mrs. J is an 85-year-old woman who recently lost her husband of 60 years. She is struggling with intense grief and feelings of loneliness and isolation. In therapy, Mrs. J reflects on her life and her relationship with her husband, as well as her own fears of death and dying. Through psychodynamic therapy, she is able to process her grief and find ways to cope with her loss and find comfort in her memories.

In both of these cases, the therapist must take into consideration the unique challenges and experiences of their elderly clients in order to provide effective therapy. By addressing these specific issues, the therapist can help their clients find a sense of fulfillment and emotional well-being in their later years.

Chapter 31: Dual Diagnosis in Psychodynamic Therapy

Dual diagnosis refers to the co-occurrence of a mental health disorder and a substance use disorder. This is a complex and challenging issue that requires a thorough understanding and sensitive treatment approach. In this chapter, we will explore the psychodynamic understanding and treatment of dual diagnosis, as well as provide case examples to illustrate the complexities of this condition.

Psychodynamic Understanding of Dual Diagnosis

As with any issue in psychodynamic therapy, understanding the underlying causes of dual diagnosis requires an exploration of the client's unconscious conflicts and past experiences. Often, individuals with dual diagnosis have a history of trauma, especially in childhood, which may have led to the development of both mental health and substance use disorders.

One of the key concepts in psychodynamic therapy is the use of defense mechanisms as a way to cope with and protect oneself from painful experiences and emotions. Individuals with dual diagnosis may rely heavily on these defenses, such as denial and rationalization, to avoid facing their underlying issues and using substances as a means of escape.

In addition, there may also be an underlying sense of emptiness or void that individuals with dual diagnosis are attempting to fill through substance use. This can be linked to early attachment wounds and a lack of emotional support and nurturing in childhood.

Treatment Approaches in Psychodynamic Therapy

Treating dual diagnosis in psychodynamic therapy can be challenging, as addressing both the mental health and substance use disorders requires a multi-faceted approach. While traditional psychoanalytic techniques such as free association and interpretation may be useful, there are also other approaches that may be beneficial in working with this population.

One important aspect of treatment is the establishment of a strong therapeutic relationship. For individuals with dual diagnosis, this can be particularly challenging due to issues with trust and attachment. However, a warm and empathetic therapist can provide a supportive and stable presence, which is necessary for any therapeutic work to be effective. Another crucial aspect of treatment is addressing the client's trauma history, as this may have contributed significantly to the development of both disorders. This may involve working through past traumatic experiences and exploring how they impact current behaviors and thought patterns.

In addition, a key component of treatment is helping the client to develop more adaptive coping strategies and healthier ways of regulating emotions. This can be done through exploring and understanding their defense mechanisms, as well as introducing new coping skills such as mindfulness techniques.

Case Examples

Samantha came to therapy seeking help for her depression and anxiety. In the course of therapy, it was revealed that she also struggled with a cocaine addiction. Through exploring her childhood experiences, Samantha realized that she had been neglected and emotionally abandoned by her parents, which left her with an overwhelming sense of emptiness and a constant need to numb her feelings with substances. Through therapy, she was able to work through her attachment wounds and develop healthier ways of managing her emotions.

Another example is John, who had a history of trauma from childhood physical and emotional abuse. He sought therapy for his struggles with alcohol and anger issues. Through therapy, it became clear that his substance use and rage were ways of masking and avoiding the deep emotional pain from his past. With the support of his therapist, John was able to confront and work through his traumatic experiences, leading to a decrease in his reliance on substances and improved anger management.

Final Thoughts

Dual diagnosis is a challenging and complex issue that requires a sensitive and comprehensive treatment approach, such as psychodynamic therapy. By understanding the root causes and addressing both the mental health and substance use disorders, individuals with dual diagnosis can find healing and a path towards recovery. As therapists, it is important to continue to educate ourselves on this topic and remain open-minded and non-judgmental when working with this population.

Chapter 32: Applying Psychodynamic Principles in Real-life Cases

Psychodynamic therapy is a highly effective approach in treating various mental health challenges. The focus of this therapeutic approach is understanding unconscious motivations that underlie and fuel our thoughts and behaviors. While the principles and techniques of psychodynamic therapy may seem abstract and theoretical, they can be applied in practical ways to real-life cases. In this chapter, we will explore the application of psychodynamic principles and techniques in real-life scenarios, along with reflections and discussions on their effectiveness.

Application of Psychodynamic Principles and Techniques to Real-life Cases

As mentioned earlier, psychodynamic therapy focuses on understanding the unconscious mind and how it influences our thoughts and behaviors. This approach is often used to treat mood disorders, anxiety disorders, and personality disorders among others. Let us take the example of a client with severe depression to understand the application of psychodynamic principles in a real-life case.

Upon initial assessment, it was observed that Jordan (name changed) had been struggling with recurrent depressive episodes since his teenage years. He had difficulty maintaining close relationships and often isolated himself from others. Jordan was also struggling with low self-esteem and feelings of worthlessness. Through psychodynamic therapy, it was revealed that Jordan had a troubled childhood, with a distant and critical father and an overprotective mother. This led to him internalizing feelings of inadequacy and worthlessness, which manifested in the form of depression.

In this scenario, the psychodynamic therapist would use techniques such as free association and interpretation to help Jordan explore his unconscious thoughts and feelings. The therapist would also focus on establishing a strong therapeutic relationship to provide a sense of safety and support for the client. By exploring the underlying causes of Jordan's depression, the therapist would help him gain insight and work through his feelings of low self-worth.

Another significant aspect of psychodynamic therapy is the use of transference. Transference refers to the tendency of clients to transfer their feelings and emotions from previous relationships onto the therapist. In the case of Jordan, he may transfer his feelings of worthlessness onto the therapist. The therapist would use this transference to guide Jordan towards resolving his internalized negative feelings and developing a healthier self-image.

Apart from individual therapy, psychodynamic principles can also be applied in couples and family therapy. Family dynamics and communication patterns are heavily influenced by unconscious thoughts and feelings, and psychodynamic therapy can help uncover and address these underlying issues. For instance, a couple struggling with conflict and resentment may discover that their communication patterns are influenced by their past experiences and expectations. By exploring these unconscious factors, they can improve their relationship and establish healthier communication patterns.

Reflection and Discussion

While psychodynamic therapy has been proven effective in treating various mental health challenges, it is not without its criticisms and controversies. One of the primary criticisms is the lack of empirical evidence in supporting its effectiveness. However, proponents of this approach argue that its focus on the individual and their unique experiences makes it difficult to measure its effectiveness through standardized measures. Another aspect to consider is the role of the therapist in psychodynamic therapy. Unlike other therapeutic approaches, the therapist in psychodynamic therapy plays a more active role, providing interpretations and insights into the client's unconscious thoughts and feelings. Some argue that this may lead to a power imbalance in the therapeutic relationship. However, proponents argue that it is necessary for the therapist to guide the client towards a deeper understanding of themselves and their underlying motivations.

In addition to these discussions, it is also essential to reflect on the cultural and historical influences on psychodynamic therapy. This approach has its roots in the works of Sigmund Freud and his contemporaries and has undergone significant changes over the years. Today, we see a more inclusive and diverse understanding of the unconscious mind and its influence on our thoughts and behaviors.

Another critical aspect to reflect on is the integration of psychodynamic therapy with other therapeutic approaches. While this approach has its unique techniques and principles, it can be integrated with other approaches such as cognitive-behavioral therapy or mindfulness-based therapy to create a more holistic and comprehensive treatment plan. It is crucial for therapists to be open to exploring these integrations to best serve their clients' needs.

Conclusion

In conclusion, psychodynamic therapy is a powerful approach in treating various mental health challenges. Its focus on understanding the unconscious mind and exploring underlying motivations provides a unique perspective that complements other therapeutic approaches. By understanding and applying psychodynamic principles and techniques in real-life cases, therapists can help their clients gain insight and work towards improving their mental health and overall well-being. However, it is crucial to continue reflecting and discussing the effectiveness of this approach as it continues to evolve and adapt to the ever-changing needs of our society.

Chapter 33: Cultural and Societal Influences on the Development of Psychodynamic Theory

Influence of Culture

Culture shapes our understanding of the world and how we relate to others. Therefore, it is inevitable that culture plays a significant role in the development of psychodynamic theory. Culture encompasses our values, beliefs, and norms, and it directly impacts our thoughts, feelings, and behaviors. In turn, our cultural background influences how we perceive ourselves and others, and how we construct our sense of self.

One of the most significant contributions of culture to psychodynamic theory is the concept of cultural relativism. This concept acknowledges that different cultures have different ways of understanding and expressing their emotions and experiences. It challenges the idea that there is a universal human experience and encourages us to view individuals within the context of their cultural background. This has led to a deeper understanding of how cultural factors can impact the therapeutic process. Another important aspect of culture in psychodynamic theory is the role of traditions and cultural practices in shaping the family dynamics and underlying psychological conflicts. For example, in cultures where collectivism is valued, there is a higher emphasis on maintaining harmony within the family, which can lead to difficulties in expressing individual needs and emotions. This may contribute to the development of certain psychological disorders, such as anxiety and depression.

Additionally, cultural differences in power dynamics, such as hierarchical structures and gender roles, can also influence the development of psychodynamic theories. For instance, in patriarchal societies, the dominant male figure may be seen as the main source of authority and power within the family, which can impact the dynamics between family members and the individuals' sense of self.

Influence of Gender

The role of gender and its impact on psychodynamic theory has been a topic of intense discussion. Traditionally, psychodynamic theory was heavily influenced by male thinkers, and it was believed that women's psychological experiences were not significantly different from men's. However, with the rise of feminism and gender studies, there has been a shift in understanding the impact of gender on psychological development.

One of the significant contributions of gender to psychodynamic theory is the concept of gender identity and its formation. Psychodynamic theory suggests that our understanding of self is largely shaped by early experiences, including our relationship with our primary caretaker. However, this concept fails to account for the unique experiences of gender non-conforming individuals and the impact of societal expectations and norms on their identity formation. Additionally, gender differences have been noted in the expression of emotions and the dynamics of relationships. Women are often socialized to be more emotionally expressive, while men are taught to suppress their emotions. This can have a significant impact on how individuals in therapy communicate and how emotions are explored within the therapeutic relationship.

Furthermore, psychodynamic theory has also been criticized for its portrayal of female sexuality as being inferior to male sexuality. It fails to consider the unique psychological and societal pressures faced by women in relation to their sexual desires and expressions. These gender biases have led to a reassessment of traditional psychodynamic theories and the development of more inclusive and diverse perspectives.

Influence of Society

Society and its norms and values play a crucial role in shaping our understanding, thoughts, and behaviors. Thus, it is essential to consider societal influences when examining psychodynamic theory. Society's influence can be seen in the development of social norms, expectations, and societal roles, which can have a significant impact on an individual's sense of self and mental health.

For example, in societies that place a high value on productivity and achievement, individuals may develop a strong internalized pressure to succeed, leading to perfectionism and anxiety. This can be particularly challenging for individuals with underlying psychodynamic conflicts, as their struggles may be amplified by external pressures.

Moreover, societal changes, such as globalization and advancements in technology, have also impacted the practice of psychodynamic therapy. With the rise of social media and the increasing availability of online therapy, therapists must consider the role of technology and its impact on the therapeutic relationship and the individual's sense of self.

Challenges and Opportunities

The influence of culture, gender, and society on the development of psychodynamic theory creates both challenges and opportunities. On one hand, it highlights the limitations of traditional psychodynamic perspectives, which were developed by Western, white, male thinkers, and calls for a more diverse and inclusive approach to understanding human psychology. On the other hand, it presents an opportunity for the field to evolve and adapt to the changing needs of our globalized and diverse society. Therapists must continuously examine their own biases and assumptions to ensure that they do not impose their cultural and societal values on their clients. This requires ongoing self-reflection and ongoing learning about diversity and cultural competence in therapy. By acknowledging and considering the impact of culture, gender, and society on psychodynamic theory, therapists can provide more effective and culturally sensitive treatment.

In conclusion, culture, gender, and society are integral to the development of psychodynamic theory. They highlight the need for a more inclusive and diverse approach to understanding human psychology and provide a framework for therapists to consider the impact of these factors on their clients. By recognizing and addressing these influences, therapists can create a more comprehensive and effective therapeutic experience for their clients.

Chapter 34: The Future of Psychodynamic Therapy

As we look towards the future of psychodynamic therapy, there are both exciting emerging trends and innovations, as well as challenges and opportunities that we must consider. In this chapter, we will explore these factors and how they may shape the practice of psychodynamic therapy in the years to come.

Emerging Trends and Innovations

One of the most exciting emerging trends in psychodynamic therapy is the integration of technology into the therapeutic process. With the rise of teletherapy and virtual therapy platforms, therapists can now connect with clients from anywhere in the world. This has opened up new possibilities for accessibility and convenience for both therapists and clients. Additionally, there is a growing interest in the use of virtual reality and artificial intelligence in therapy, which may offer more immersive and personalized experiences for clients. Another trend that is gaining traction is the combination of psychodynamic therapy with other evidence-based approaches, such as cognitive-behavioral therapy (CBT) or mindfulness-based interventions. This integrative approach allows therapists to draw from multiple theories and techniques to create a more tailored and effective treatment plan for each individual client.

In recent years, there has also been a renewed interest in the role of attachment theory in psychodynamic therapy. With a deeper understanding of how early childhood experiences shape our relationships and behaviors, therapists are incorporating attachment-focused interventions into their treatment approaches. This is particularly relevant in working with clients who may have experienced trauma or have attachment-related struggles in their current relationships.

Challenges and Opportunities

As with any field, there are also challenges that must be addressed in the future of psychodynamic therapy. One of the main challenges is the continued need for empirical research to support the effectiveness of psychodynamic therapy. While there is a growing body of evidence, there is still a need for more rigorous studies and data to validate the efficacy of this approach.

Another challenge is the increasing cost of therapy and the barriers to access for those who cannot afford it. This is a concern that applies to the mental health field as a whole, and it is essential to consider ways to make psychodynamic therapy more accessible to those who may benefit from it. However, with these challenges also comes the opportunity for growth and change. There is a growing awareness of the importance of mental health and the need for effective treatment modalities. This can create opportunities for therapists to increase collaboration with other mental health professionals and advocate for policies that promote mental health and wellness in our communities.

As we move towards a more diverse and globalized society, there is also an opportunity for psychodynamic therapy to address cultural considerations and provide culturally sensitive treatment to a wider range of clients. This will require therapists to continually educate themselves on various cultural backgrounds and adapt their approach accordingly.

In terms of education and training, there is an opportunity for creative and innovative programs that support the development of competent and ethical psychodynamic therapists. This may involve incorporating different modalities, such as experiential learning, to enhance the learning experience and better prepare therapists for real-world situations. Furthermore, there is an opportunity for increased collaboration and integration across different theoretical and therapeutic approaches. As we continue to study the complexity of the human mind, it becomes evident that no single theory or approach can fully explain and address all psychological struggles. By working together and drawing from multiple perspectives, we can create a more holistic and effective approach to therapy.

Unconventional Approaches and Perspectives

Looking even further into the future of psychodynamic therapy, there may be room for unconventional and creative approaches that challenge traditional ways of thinking and practicing. One such approach is utilizing the arts, such as music, dance, or visual arts, as a form of expression and healing in therapy. This can be particularly beneficial for clients who struggle with verbal communication or have experienced trauma that is difficult to verbalize. Additionally, as our understanding of the brain and the human mind continues to expand, there may be new and unconventional techniques or interventions that arise. This could include the use of psychedelics for therapeutic purposes or the development of technology that enhances the therapeutic process.

In Conclusion

The future of psychodynamic therapy is full of possibilities and potential for growth and development. By acknowledging the emerging trends and innovations, as well as the challenges and opportunities, we can work towards creating a more dynamic and effective practice for the benefit of our clients. As therapists, it is our responsibility to continually educate ourselves and adapt our approaches to best serve those who come to us seeking help and healing.

Chapter 35: The Importance of Continuing Education and Personal Growth as a Psychodynamic Therapist

The Journey of a Psychodynamic Therapist

Psychodynamic therapy is a complex and ever-evolving approach to psychotherapy. Rooted in the works of prominent figures such as Freud, Jung, and Adler, it has been continuously shaped by different schools of thought and critical analyses. As a result, it has become a comprehensive, eclectic, and versatile approach to understanding the human mind and providing therapeutic interventions. But what makes a psychodynamic therapist effective and successful in their practice? What separates a good therapist from a great one? The answer lies in the lifelong commitment to learning and personal growth.

The Ever-Changing Landscape of Psychology

As a discipline, psychology is constantly evolving. New research, theories, and techniques are emerging every day, challenging our existing beliefs and offering new perspectives. As psychodynamic therapists, it is our responsibility to stay abreast of these developments and continuously integrate them into our practice. This means engaging in lifelong learning and seeking out opportunities for growth and professional development.

The Value of Continuing Education

Continuing education is an essential aspect of being a successful psychodynamic therapist. It involves participating in activities such as workshops, conferences, seminars, and courses to enhance one's knowledge, skills, and abilities in the field of psychology. These opportunities provide a platform for therapists to connect with their colleagues, share their experiences, and gain new insights into the various aspects of their practice. It also allows them to stay current with the latest research, treatment techniques, and ethical standards to ensure that they are providing their clients with the best possible care.

Personal Growth and Self-Reflection

While continuing education is imperative for professional growth, personal growth is equally important. As therapists, we are constantly working with individuals who have experienced adversity, trauma, and emotional distress in their lives. It is crucial that we take care of our own emotional and mental well-being to better support our clients. Engaging in regular self-reflection, seeking therapy for ourselves, and pursuing activities that bring us joy and fulfillment are all key components of personal growth. By tending to our own needs, we can show up as better versions of ourselves in our therapeutic practice.

The Role of Supervision

Supervision is an invaluable tool for a therapist's professional development and personal growth. It allows therapists to reflect on their practice, receive feedback from their peers and supervisors, and identify areas for improvement. It also serves as a forum to discuss challenging cases and ethical issues and receive guidance on how to navigate them effectively. Seeking supervision shows a commitment to being a lifelong learner and continuously striving to improve as a therapist.

Exploring New Approaches and Techniques

The field of psychodynamic therapy is not limited to the traditional approach of Freudian psychoanalysis. Over the years, many new schools of thought have emerged, such as Attachment Theory, Object Relations Theory, and Self-Psychology, which have expanded our understanding of the human psyche and the therapeutic process. As psychodynamic therapists, it is essential to explore and incorporate these different approaches and techniques into our practice. This allows us to tailor our interventions to best suit our clients' unique needs and provide more effective and individualized care.

Staying Culturally Competent

Cultural competence is vital in the field of psychology, particularly in today's diverse and interconnected world. As psychodynamic therapists, it is crucial to recognize and value the influence of culture, race, ethnicity, and other intersecting identities on an individual's experiences and mental health. Therefore, striving to increase cultural competence is an ongoing process that involves developing an awareness of our own biases, attitudes, and cultural upbringing. It also requires us to stay informed about different cultures and identities and integrate this knowledge into our practice.

The Importance of Reflection and Creative Expression

Psychodynamic therapy is a deeply personal and profound experience for both the therapist and the client. It requires therapists to be introspective, open-minded, and empathic, which can be emotionally draining at times. Therefore, it is crucial to regularly engage in activities that promote self-reflection and creative expression. This could include journaling, art, music, or other forms of creative outlets that allow us to process our emotions and recharge our mental and emotional batteries.

The Impact on the Therapist-Client Relationship

As psychodynamic therapists, we recognize the therapeutic relationship as a crucial factor in the success of our work. The therapist-client relationship is built on trust, empathy, and mutual understanding. By committing to our own personal growth and continuous education, we can become more self-aware and better attuned to our clients' needs. This allows us to establish a strong therapeutic alliance and create a safe and supportive space for our clients to heal and grow.

Conclusion

The journey of a psychodynamic therapist is one of continuous learning, growth, and self-discovery. It requires a commitment to personal and professional development, cultural competence, and ongoing reflection. As we embark on this journey, we not only better ourselves as therapists but also improve the lives of our clients and contribute to the ever-changing landscape of psychology. Therefore, let us continue to prioritize our growth and development, for the benefit of ourselves and those we serve.

Chapter 36: Contributions of Other Theorists to Psychodynamic Therapy

Jungian, Adlerian and Object Relations Theories

As we delve deeper into the world of psychodynamic therapy, it is important to acknowledge the contributions of other prominent theorists who have shaped this field. Sigmund Freud may be considered the father of psychodynamic theory, but he was not the only one who paved the way for this approach to therapy. In this chapter, we will explore the work of three notable figures in the world of psychology: Carl Jung, Alfred Adler, and object relations theorists.

While Freudian theory focused on the role of the unconscious and childhood experiences, Jungian psychology emphasized the concept of the collective unconscious, which he believed to be a shared pool of archetypes and innate psychological patterns that influence our thoughts, emotions, and behaviors. According to Jung, by tapping into the collective unconscious, individuals can gain a deeper understanding of themselves and their place in the world. This idea of a collective unconscious has been widely accepted and integrated into the practice of psychodynamic therapy.

Adlerian theory, on the other hand, emphasized the role of social and environmental factors in shaping an individual's personality. Adler believed that our drive for superiority and striving for success were influenced by our early experiences and the expectations of society. He also introduced the concept of the inferiority complex, which he suggested was a universal feeling of inadequacy that can drive individuals to strive for perfection. This theory has been integrated into psychodynamic therapy, helping therapists to understand the impact of social and cultural influences on their clients.

Another influential school of thought that emerged in the psychodynamic landscape is object relations theory, which focuses on the relationship between the individual and their significant others, particularly in childhood. Object relations theorists believe that our early attachment experiences shape our relationships and personalities in adulthood. This theory has been valuable in understanding the dynamics in therapy, as transference and countertransference are commonly explored in the therapeutic relationship.

Comparison with Freudian Theory

While Freudian theory laid the foundation for psychodynamic therapy, many of these later theories have challenged and expanded upon his ideas. One major difference between Freudian and Jungian theory, for example, is the concept of the collective unconscious. While Freud emphasized personal unconscious thoughts and experiences, Jung brought a more holistic approach to understanding the human mind. Adler's focus on social and environmental factors also diverged from Freud's emphasis on the drives of the individual. Additionally, object relations theorists have shifted the focus from sexual and aggressive drives to the importance of early relationships and attachment experiences. Despite these differences, all of these theories share the belief that our childhood experiences and unconscious thoughts play a significant role in shaping our behaviors and patterns in adulthood. They also recognize the importance of the therapeutic relationship in exploring and resolving these underlying issues.

Uncommon Yet Important Concepts

As we continue to explore these theories, it is essential to note the unique and valuable concepts they have brought to the practice of psychodynamic therapy. Jung's idea of the collective unconscious allows for a deeper understanding of the universal archetypes and patterns that shape our experiences. Adler's concept of the inferiority complex helps therapists understand the driving forces behind their clients' behaviors and the influence of societal expectations. Object relations theory brings the focus onto the therapeutic relationship and the impact of early attachment experiences on our current relationships.

These concepts have not only expanded our understanding of the human mind and behavior but have also allowed for a more holistic and individualized approach to therapy.

Critiques and Controversies

No theory is without its critics, and the same is true for these contributions to psychodynamic therapy. Some have questioned the validity of Jung's collective unconscious and its role in shaping our experiences. Others have argued that Adler's emphasis on social factors neglects the importance of individual drives and desires. Object relations theory has also faced criticism, with some suggesting that it oversimplifies the complexities of attachment and relationships.

However, regardless of these critiques, it cannot be denied that these theories have significantly contributed to the development and evolution of psychodynamic therapy. They have expanded our understanding of the human mind and provided valuable insights and techniques for therapists to use in their practice. As with any theory, it is essential to critically evaluate and integrate these concepts into our practice, taking into consideration the unique needs and experiences of each individual client.

The Future of Psychodynamic Therapy

As we look to the future of psychodynamic therapy, it is evident that the contributions of these other theorists will continue to shape and influence the field. We have already seen an integration of these theories into the practice of psychodynamic therapy, and it is likely that this will only continue to grow. The emphasis on the therapeutic relationship, attachment experiences, and cultural influences has become paramount in the practice of psychodynamic therapy, and it is these contributions that have made it possible.

Professional Development and Self-Reflection

As therapists, it is crucial that we continue to seek out new knowledge and understandings of the human mind and behavior. This involves not only staying updated on the latest research and theories but also engaging in self-reflection and personal growth. Engaging in ongoing professional development, seeking out supervision and consultation, and actively engaging in self-reflection can help us to continually integrate new concepts and perspectives into our practice. By doing so, we can better serve our clients and continue to evolve as therapists.

Conclusion

In conclusion, the contributions of other theorists have been vital in shaping the world of psychodynamic therapy. Jung, Adler, and object relations theorists have expanded our understanding of the human mind and behavior, bringing new concepts and perspectives to the field. While they may have their differences and controversies, it is undeniable that their contributions have been significant in helping individuals and therapists alike to gain a deeper understanding of themselves and the world around them. As we continue to strive for growth and progress in the field of psychodynamic therapy, it is essential to acknowledge and appreciate the contributions of these theorists and continue to integrate their ideas into our practice.

Chapter 37: Critiques and Controversies in Psychodynamic Therapy

Psychodynamic therapy has been practiced for over a century, and its impact on the field of clinical psychology cannot be denied. While it has evolved and adapted over the years, it continues to be a controversial approach, with critics questioning its effectiveness and validity. In this chapter, we will explore some of the critiques and controversies surrounding psychodynamic therapy, as well as the empirical evidence that supports or challenges its theory and practice.

Empirical Evidence

One of the main criticisms of psychodynamic therapy is the lack of empirical evidence to support its effectiveness. Critics argue that the approach relies heavily on personal interpretation rather than empirical data, making it difficult to measure its outcomes. However, several studies have been conducted to examine the effectiveness of psychodynamic therapy, and the results are quite promising.

One meta-analysis found that psychodynamic therapy was equally effective as other forms of therapy, such as cognitive-behavioral therapy, in treating a variety of mental health issues. Another study found that psychodynamic therapy had a significant positive effect on reducing symptoms of depression, anxiety, and personality disorders. Additionally, a long-term follow-up study found that the benefits of psychodynamic therapy lasted well beyond the end of treatment.

These studies suggest that psychodynamic therapy is indeed effective and can produce long-lasting results for clients. It also supports the idea that the therapeutic relationship, a cornerstone of psychodynamic therapy, plays a significant role in healing and change.

Challenges to Psychodynamic Theory and Practice

While there is empirical support for the effectiveness of psychodynamic therapy, there are also challenges to its theory and practice. One of the main criticisms is the focus on past experiences and childhood trauma, which some argue may lead to victim-blaming and the neglect of current issues. Critics also question the validity of concepts such as the unconscious and defense mechanisms, arguing that they are difficult to measure and may not have a scientific basis.

Another challenge is the lack of diversity in psychodynamic theory. Early pioneers of the approach, such as Sigmund Freud, were white men from a specific cultural and socio-economic background. The theories and techniques they developed may not be applicable to clients from different backgrounds, and research has shown that cultural competency is essential in providing effective therapy. The field has made efforts to address this issue, but there is still work to be done in diversifying psychodynamic theory and practice.

The therapeutic relationship is integral to psychodynamic therapy, and while it can be profoundly healing, it also presents challenges. Boundaries and transference are often a hot topic in discussions of psychodynamic therapy. Critics suggest that the power dynamics inherent in the therapeutic relationship can be damaging and perpetuate unhealthy dynamics. Additionally, some argue that transference may lead to a perpetuation of the client's relational patterns rather than true healing.

The Role of the Therapist

Another area of controversy in psychodynamic therapy is the role of the therapist. Freud believed that the therapist should remain a blank slate, with minimal self-disclosure and a focus on interpretation. However, many modern practitioners encourage a more active role for the therapist, involving self-disclosure, guidance, and support. This disagreement on the role of the therapist can lead to confusion for clients and the therapist alike, and there is little consensus among practitioners.

New Directions in Psychodynamic Therapy

Psychodynamic therapy continues to evolve and adapt, and new approaches are gaining popularity in the field. Modern psychodynamic theories, such as attachment theory and object relations theory, have expanded on Freud's original ideas and integrated new concepts and techniques. These approaches also place a greater emphasis on the therapeutic relationship and the client's current experiences.

Another exciting direction in psychodynamic therapy is the integration of neuroscience. Recent research on the brain has shed light on some of the mechanisms behind psychodynamic concepts, such as the unconscious and defense mechanisms. This integration may help bridge the gap between psychodynamic theory and empirical evidence and provide a deeper understanding of how psychoanalysis works.

The Impact of Critiques and Controversies

While criticisms and controversies may challenge traditional psychodynamic theory and practice, they also have a valuable role in shaping the field and promoting growth and adaptation. As the field continues to evolve, it is essential to critically examine the approach and integrate new ideas and perspectives. The ongoing dialogue and debate can lead to a better understanding of psychodynamic therapy and its effectiveness.

Closing Thoughts

The critiques and controversies surrounding psychodynamic therapy serve as a reminder that no approach is perfect or exempt from criticism. However, the empirical evidence supports its effectiveness, and the approach continues to evolve and adapt to meet the needs of clients. As clinicians, it is crucial to be open to criticism and actively work towards incorporating new ideas and perspectives into our practice to provide the best possible care for our clients.

Chapter 38: The Role of Therapist's Personal Experiences and Narrative in Therapy

The Therapist's Personal Experiences: A Source of Insight and Connection

Therapists are often seen as the experts in the therapeutic relationship, equipped with knowledge and skills to help their clients navigate through their struggles. However, what is often overlooked is the importance of the therapist's own personal experiences and narratives in the therapeutic process.

As Carl Jung famously said, "Only the wounded healer can truly heal." This highlights the idea that therapists' personal experiences and wounds can serve as a source of insight and connection with their clients. When therapists are able to draw from their own lived experiences, they are better able to empathize with their clients and understand the complexities of their struggles. This can lead to a deeper level of understanding and connection between therapist and client.

Moreover, therapists' personal experiences can also inform their clinical work and theoretical understanding. Through their own experiences, therapists can gain insights into the human psyche and the universal struggles that we all face. This allows therapists to approach their work with a deeper understanding and a more nuanced perspective, ultimately benefiting their clients.

The Power of Shared Experience

One of the most powerful aspects of therapy is the opportunity to share one's experiences with another person. In the role of the therapist, this is often reversed, with the client sharing their experiences while the therapist listens and guides. However, the therapist's ability to share their own experiences can be equally impactful for the client.

In fact, some theoretical approaches, such as Narrative Therapy, highlight the value of the therapist's sharing their own stories with clients. This creates a sense of mutual understanding and can serve to normalize the client's experiences. It also allows the therapist to model vulnerability and authenticity, creating a safe and genuine space for the client to do the same.

Unpacking Unconscious Biases and Countertransference

Therapists are not immune to unconscious biases and countertransference, which can greatly impact the therapeutic relationship. By reflecting on their own personal experiences and biases, therapists can gain a better understanding of how these may be influencing their interactions with clients.

For example, a therapist who has experienced childhood trauma may have a particularly strong reaction to a client's disclosure of their own trauma. By recognizing this personal bias, the therapist can then work through it and approach the client's experiences with more objectivity and empathy.

The Therapeutic Narrative: Co-creating a Healing Story

The therapeutic process can also be seen as a co-creation of a healing narrative between the therapist and client. Through the therapist's guidance and support, the client is able to revise and reframe their understanding of their personal narrative, ultimately leading to growth and healing.

Helping Clients Challenge Dominant Narratives

Many clients come into therapy with deeply ingrained narratives of themselves and their experiences, often perpetuated by societal norms and expectations. These narratives can be limiting and harmful, leading to feelings of inadequacy and self-doubt.

As therapists, our personal experiences can help us challenge these dominant narratives and offer alternative perspectives. By sharing our own stories of overcoming adversity or challenging societal norms, we can inspire hope and encourage clients to question and deconstruct their own narratives.

Honoring the Client's Unique Story

At the same time, therapists must also recognize the importance of honoring the client's unique story. It is not our role to impose our own beliefs and narratives onto our clients, but rather to listen and guide as they shape their own understanding of their experiences.

Through our own personal experiences, therapists can better understand the complexity of individual narratives and the impact of various intersecting identities. This allows us to approach our work with cultural competence and sensitivity, ensuring that our clients feel seen and heard in their unique experiences.

Making Meaning Out of Suffering

One of the main goals of therapy is to help individuals find meaning and purpose in their suffering. This can be a daunting task, but our own personal experiences can serve as a source of hope and inspiration for our clients.

When we share our own stories of struggle and growth, we offer a sense of possibility to our clients. We show them that it is possible to make sense out of pain and to use it as a catalyst for personal growth and transformation.

Cultivating Self-Awareness and Growth as a Therapist

As therapists, it is essential that we continuously reflect on our own personal experiences and narratives. Not only does this benefit our clients, but it also allows us to cultivate self-awareness and growth in our own lives.

Taking Care of Our Own Mental Health

It is not uncommon for therapists to experience burnout and compassion fatigue, given the emotionally demanding nature of our work. By reflecting on our own personal experiences and narratives, we can better understand how our work is impacting our mental health and take steps to prioritize self-care.

Continued Learning and Development

In order to be effective therapists, it is imperative that we continue to learn and grow in our personal and professional lives. Our own experiences serve as a powerful source of learning and development, allowing us to continuously refine and improve our practice.

By embracing our own personal narratives and using them to inform our work, we not only become better therapists, but also lead more fulfilling and authentic lives.

The Beautiful Intersection of Personal and Professional

The integration of personal experiences and narratives into therapy serves to blur the lines between personal and professional. This can be seen as a beautiful thing, as therapists are able to bring their authentic selves into their work, creating a more genuine and meaningful therapeutic relationship.

In a field that values objectivity and boundaries, the inclusion of our own personal narratives may feel uncomfortable at first. However, it is essential that we recognize the power and potential in embracing our personal experiences, as this ultimately benefits both ourselves and our clients.

A Final Note

In conclusion, the role of the therapist's personal experiences and narrative in therapy cannot be underestimated. As therapists, our personal experiences serve as a source of insight, connection, and growth, both for ourselves and our clients. By embracing our personal narratives and integrating them into our work, we create a more meaningful and authentic therapeutic experience for all.

Chapter 39: Personal Narratives and Personal Experience in Psychodynamic Therapy

Impact of Traumatic Events on Therapists

As therapists, we are taught to be empathetic and compassionate towards our clients. However, what happens when our own personal experiences and traumatic events start to intersect with our professional role? The truth is, working in the field of clinical psychology can sometimes take a toll on our mental and emotional well-being, especially when we have our own unresolved traumas to contend with.

Being exposed to the raw and often painful experiences of our clients can trigger our own unresolved issues, leading to feelings of burnout, compassion fatigue, and even secondary trauma. This can be especially true for therapists who have experienced similar traumas to those of their clients. For example, a therapist who has experienced sexual abuse may find it challenging to work with clients who have also experienced sexual abuse.

It's important for therapists to recognize how their own personal histories and traumas can impact their work and overall wellness. Ignoring or burying these issues can lead to negative consequences for both the therapist and their clients. It takes courage and self-awareness to acknowledge and address these personal experiences, but it is essential for maintaining a healthy and effective therapeutic relationship.

Coping Strategies

So how can therapists cope with their own traumas and continue to provide effective therapy for their clients? One helpful coping strategy is to engage in regular self-care practices and prioritize one's own mental and emotional well-being. This can include activities like exercise, meditation or mindfulness practices, journaling, spending time in nature, or seeking support from a therapist or support group.

Another important coping strategy is maintaining healthy boundaries. It's essential for therapists to separate their personal experiences from their clients' experiences and to not take on their clients' traumas as their own. This can be challenging, especially for therapists who have experienced similar traumas, but it's crucial for maintaining objectivity and preventing burnout. Using art and creativity as an outlet can also be a powerful coping strategy for therapists. Through art, therapists can express and process their emotions in a safe and cathartic way. It can also serve as a reminder of their own resilience and strength.

Resilience

Resilience is the ability to bounce back from adversity and challenges. It's an essential characteristic for therapists to possess, as they are often faced with difficult and emotionally taxing situations. But it's also something that can be strengthened and cultivated over time.

One way to cultivate resilience is by engaging in reflective practices. This can include regularly reflecting on our experiences as therapists, our personal growth, and lessons learned. Reflecting on our own personal narratives and identifying our own strengths and resources can also contribute to our resilience. Another factor that contributes to resilience is social support. It's important for therapists to have a strong support system of friends, family, colleagues, and mentors who they can turn to for guidance and reassurance. Additionally, connecting with other therapists and participating in peer supervision can provide a sense of camaraderie and support within the field.

Lastly, having a sense of purpose and meaning in our work can significantly impact our resilience as therapists. Understanding the impact that we can have on the lives of our clients and recognizing the growth and progress they make can bring a sense of fulfillment and renewal.

In conclusion, personal narratives and personal experiences are essential elements of psychodynamic therapy. They not only help to shape the therapist's perspective and understanding of their clients, but they also play a role in the therapist's personal growth and well-being. By acknowledging and addressing the impact of traumatic events on therapists, utilizing effective coping strategies, and cultivating resilience, therapists can continue to provide effective therapy and develop a deeper understanding of themselves and their clients.

Printed in Dunstable, United Kingdom